Perr

THE BARDS OF BROMLEY AND OTHER PLAYS

Foreword by Maureen Lipman

The Three Seagulls

The Lunchtime of the Gods

The Bards of Bromley

OBERON BOOKS
LONDON

WWW.OBERONBOOKS.COM

First published in 2013 by Oberon Books Ltd
521 Caledonian Road, London N7 9RH
Tel: +44 (0) 20 7607 3637 / Fax: +44 (0) 20 7607 3629
e-mail: info@oberonbooks.com
www.oberonbooks.com

A catalogue record for this book is available from the British
Library.

PB ISBN: 978-1-84943-427-0
E ISBN: 978-1-84943-777-6

Cover illustration © James Illman

Printed, bound and converted
by CPI Group (UK) Ltd, Croydon, CR0 4YY.

THE BARDS OF BROMLEY
AND OTHER PLAYS

For Richard Wortley

Contents

Foreword

I was first introduced to the work of a young American playwright, in 1972, by the distinguished critic and writer, Kenneth Tynan. He arranged a play-reading at the Old Vic, of Perry Pontac's early play *The Old Man's Comforts*. The reading was cast from amongst Sir Laurence Olivier's National Theatre Company, one of whom was a twenty-six year old me. The other readers were David Ryall, Benjamin Whitrow, Harry Lomax and Louise Purnell.

The play was Congreve crossed with Ben Travers, a distinctive voice cutting across the zeitgeist as if the kitchen sink had never left the kitchen. I was not alone in thinking that a new writing star had been born. Time has passed, his plays have been lauded on radio and applauded on stage in *The Shakespeare Revue*, and Perry has lived in his adopted land – of Streatham, ever since. Trends have ebbed and flowed ever since but he has remained constant to a stylish mixture of parody, high comedy, flowing elegance and deep irony.

His radio plays are collector's items and his fans include Tom Stoppard and Alan Bennett. Actors, from Geraldine McEwan, John Moffatt, Harriet Walter and Julia McKenzie, to a younger generation including Simon Russell Beale and Samuel West clamour to be in his plays. His Shakespeare and Wilde parodies have cult status and his true aficionados will quote the most memorable of his lines across dressing rooms and bistro tables throughout the land.

In his revue sketch, *Othello in Earnest*, a stunning fusion of Shakespeare and Wilde, Lady Brabantio enquires of the mighty Moor as to his origins. Othello, the soldier, earnestly replies that he was born in a desert camp, where his doughty mama gave birth to him on a sandbag. Lady Brabantio's response is: 'A Sandbag?'.

In the first of these new plays, *The Three Seagulls*, Perry takes his profound knowledge of and respect for Anton Chekhov and creates an hilarious combo of *The Cherry Orchard*, *Uncle Vanya*, *The Seagull* and *The Three Sisters* which manages to be both accurate and ridiculous, while still being rather touching. All the loss and longing and self-absorption are there in empty Olga and vapid Madame Arkardina but just carried to the edge of farce. It's very funny on a page but it just screams for what Tamsin Greig and Eileen Atkins might do to it on a stage.

In *The Lunchtime of the Gods*, a fruity couple, Fraulein Lashmitz and Herr Hazenbrauer (think, as played on radio, Prunella Scales and Peter Jeffrey) relish a gargantuan meal in a German restaurant on the Rhine, whilst discussing the origins of a particularly unusual ring worn by Herr Hazenbrauer. Having established their appetites, all that happens next is the matter-of-fact telling of the plot of *The Ring* whilst waiting for the waiter to bring the next course of pig's trotters with Sauerbraten in fresh bowel grease or 'gugelhupf with almonds and a dozen spitzbuben.' The play takes one unusual twist after another and ends with a splash and a little Wagner played on conch shells.

In *The Bards of Bromley*, Pontac mines the territory of the creative writers' workshop, now rapidly overtaking Am-Dram and fishing as the number-one hobby of our times. Here we find our tremulous tutor, the barely published Mrs. Swerdlow, giving writing assessments to a small gathering of authors, namely Johann Wolfgang von Goethe, William Wordsworth, August Strindberg, George Eliot and A.A. Milne, in present-day Bromley. Perry knows all their voices intimately, makes them all behave utterly in character and the result is mischief and mayhem.

Perry may be from California – indeed from Tinseltown itself, and may have a name like an early twentieth-century car, but his style is English to the 'Cor'. He writes comfortably in iambic pentameter, sweeping Wagnerian phrases or heightened nineteenth-century prose. He's delighted by his own naughtiness and he makes a gift to the reader of that delight. Roll it from your eyes to your tongue, like tears, and relish, as I do, the ever-so-fruity yet slightly salty content.

Maureen Lipman, 2013

THE THREE SEAGULLS

a Chekhovian comedy

Characters

DR. ASTROV

OLGA

MADAME ARKADINA

TROFIMOV

FIRS

The drawing room of a house on a country estate in pre-revolutionary Russia. OLGA sits knitting near the samovar. DR. ASTROV stands musing and smoking a pipe. Melancholy balalaika music, which fades away as DR. ASTROV speaks.

DR ASTROV: My dear Olga, my sweet Olechna Nazarovna, I've known you for over twenty years, from the first time I visited this house. I was only a young man then, not a middle-aged doctor with an interest in forestry as I am now. And you were just a child. And your mother Alexandra Irina Nostrinska Arkadina – a lovely woman then as now.

OLGA: True, Dr Astrov. My dear Siminsky Chebatykin Ivanivich, would you like some tea? The samovar is just aboil.

DR ASTROV: Tea? Ah, thank you, Olga Michnovia Petrovna. How well I remember tea and piroshkies in your grandfather's time – dear Dimitri Ivanov Ilyich Rasnovsky – happy days round the singing samovar.

OLGA makes tea.

Languishing all morning in the summerhouse, listening to your old nurse Marina strumming the balalaika beneath the autumn trees. And philosophising, always philosophising.

OLGA: Yes, Doctor.

DR ASTROV: Your dear grandfather was blessed with three sisters as I recall, and each of them had a seagull that used to roost in their Uncle Vanya's cherry orchard. *(With a sigh.)* All flown away now – the seagulls I mean, like symbols of happier times. And your grandfather and his sisters and their uncle… gone as well, passing on to a better place

God be praised. The orchard still stands and the great forest beyond, and you yet have this old house of memories. But for how long?

OLGA:

Don't bother yourself so, Dr Astrov, kind Fiodor Orlovsky Trepliov. Life changes, life must change, but God who is changeless watches over all.

She passes him his tea and dumplings on a plate.

Here's your tea – and some beetroot dumplings.

DR ASTROV:

Thank you so much, Anya Lubichova. Beetroot dumplings. How well I remember your Aunt Zlubovskina's dumplings. Your father so loved them. *(He sips his tea.)*

OLGA:

Yes.

DR ASTROV:

And when is your mother, dear Madame Arkadina, going to arrive? It must be a long ride to the countryside – all the way from Moscow.

A pause.

OLGA:

(Yearningly.) Moscow. Moscow. Moscow.

DR ASTROV:

Ever been?

OLGA:

(Sadly.) No. Not for years and years and years.

DR ASTROV:

My poor Olgavinskya. A wonderful place, Moscow. Theatres, palaces, universities, restaurants, ballrooms, all-night cabbage shops. You should seriously think about going some day. *(Impulsively.)* Perhaps you could leave on the next train. I'll take you to the station myself – in my troika. *(Realising.)* Ah, but then you would miss your dear mother on her annual visit here. I talk so foolishly.

OLGA: You're a kind-hearted man, Michail Kavinovich Plutovsky, a very kind-hearted man. But the world itself isn't always kind. It would be if it could, I feel. But there's darkness in the very air, in the roots of trees, in the crystal waves of the sea, in the shadowy depths of caves.

DR ASTROV: *(Drinking tea.)* Darkness in shadowy caves – yes, I see that.

OLGA: And in the soul of man. But beneath that, all is light I am sure, Dr Astrov – a great brightness yearning to break free and illuminate all of life and its goodness. Like beams of morning piercing the dark sky, or lumps of soured cream dissolving in borscht. *(Embarrassed.)* I'm talking nonsense I know. Forgive me, Dr Astrov.

DR ASTROV: No, not at all. Besides, I often talk nonsense myself, Sonyaskya Zipuvina. Or so your mother often used to say. And soon she will be with us again – dear Irina Natalia Arkadina. It's been so long.

The door opens. TROFIMOV enters.

TROFIMOV: Good morning, Doctor.

DR ASTROV: Good morning, Piotr Trofimov. Have you come to welcome Madame Arkadina?

TROFIMOV: Yes. *(With ardour.)* Good morning, my dear Olga Michnovia.

OLGA: *(Frostily.)* Trofimov.

TROFIMOV: Don't be so cool towards me, Olgavina Varya. You know how I feel about you.

OLGA: *(Embarrassed.)* Please, Trofimov.

TROFIMOV: Ah, isn't she beautiful, Astrov? Not to look at perhaps, but she has a beautiful soul, as beautiful as the soul of Mother Russia, as pure as the snow on the Caucasus, and as noble as the great trees of our forests. Oh, my darling Olga, marry me and come away with me. We shall live in a rude hut by a swamp. And we shall work, Olga Petrovna, work all the day and all the night in the fields – toiling and sweating and bending until our bodies are stiff and aching and covered with welts and sores. Think of it, my darling.

OLGA: Do go away, Trofimov. You're a good man, but over the years you've changed. You used to be handsome and refined looking. Now you wear wire spectacles, your hair is thin and unruly, your moustache is untrimmed and tobacco-stained. You dress like a peasant, you smell like a pig – several pigs sometimes.

TROFIMOV: These things are of no importance at all, dear Olganiska. You're a schoolteacher – surely you understand. *(To ASTROV.)* Don't you agree, Astrov? It's the *inner* man that matters. Only the man who cares not for himself can care for others. Society must be changed; we must consider the generations yet to come, the ultimate hopes of mankind, the new Russia about to be born.

DR ASTROV: *(With relish.)* Philosophising? Ah, good, Piotr Sergeyivich. For myself, I should say that the true path to enlightenment can be found only…

(The jingle of sleigh bells.)

I'm afraid we haven't time, my dear fellow. I hear the sound of sleigh bells. Madame Arkadina has arrived.

OLGA: Mamma. *(Loudly.)* Firs! Oh, Firs!

FIRS enters, an ancient retainer somewhat overdressed.

FIRS: Yes, Mistress?

OLGA:	My mother is here. Bring in her things please, and take care of the horses.
FIRS:	Yes, Olga Anyisa. I've been a servant here for more than sixty-five years. I'm an old man now, but I can still carry a few trunks and cases and chests up the stairs, God be praised, and unharness and stable a team of horses.

FIRS goes off.

TROFIMOV:	And I shall go and help with the hatboxes. Excuse me, Doctor. Dear Olga Nublivska.

TROFIMOV exits.

DR ASTROV:	Pyetia Trofimov is a kind, decent man, Olga, and he's very fond of you. He's not at all presentable of course, but he has a good soul and an even temper and he would make a loyal, hard-working husband.
OLGA:	I know, Dr Astrov. He is a fine man. But my heart…my heart belongs to another… who knows it not. My heart belongs to… *(With yearning passion.)* Oh, Dr Astrov… my dear Lumivich Petraski Yublov…my sweet Plutzykin Semionivich…my wonderful Alexandrovsky Bukaloff…
DR ASTROV:	Yes?

The door opens. TROFIMOV, carrying some hat boxes, enters with MADAME ARKADINA.

TROFIMOV:	She's here! Madame Arkadina has returned.
DR ASTROV:	My dear Irina Nikolayevna. Welcome home dearest lady!

He kisses her hand.

ARKADINA:	Thank you, Doctor. Ah, dear house, dear chimneypiece, dear coalscuttle, dear drinks

	cabinet, dear old samovar. And – dear little Olga, in her sweet little apron and dust-cap.
OLGA:	Mamma!

MADAME ARKADINA and OLGA embrace and kiss.

ARKADINA: My darling girl. *(To the company.)* My friends. It's so good to be with 'civilised' people again.

Flattered, the others laugh with delight.

I rode here on the train with a vile ex-peasant named Ferapopopov – a businessman who talked and ate radishes all the way from Moscow. I told him of my debts and showed him my accounts, and he said I must sell some portion of my estate – the summerhouse and the area round it at the very least.

OLGA gasps.

He mentioned something about…an auction, I believe.

OLGA: But, Mamma, surely you didn't…

ARKADINA: It was foolish I know, but I'm afraid I took pity on him and…made him my business manager. Oh, but let's not talk of this. It's so good to be back, my dear ones. Moscow is exciting of course, stately and cosmopolitan, with a great surge of life, the heart of Mother Russia to which all arteries lead.

OLGA: *(Yearningly.)* Oh, Moscow. Moscow, Moscow.

ARKADINA: But this is home. This is the countryside, the living soul of the Motherland. This is the chalice of my youth. *(Weepingly.)* Oh, my dear house, my beloved wallpaper, dear door handles, blesséd chandelier that shone so brightly on my childish play, my sweet hours of vacant ease and innocence and joy, before I knew the dark pain of later life, the cruel shadow of frustration and despair. *(Sadly.)* Oh, my dear friends.

Everyone is weeping now.

TROFIMOV: Dear Anya Irina Petrovna Nikoleyevna...

DR ASTROV: My dear Trofimov, let me embrace you.

TROFIMOV: And I you, Doctor, my dear Siminsky Ivanivich Caruthers.

ASTROV and TROFIMOV embrace.

OLGA: And I you, Mamma.

ARKADINA: And I you, my dear Olga, my precious Olechka. Forgive a mother her tears.

OLGA: *(Sobbing.)* Oh, Mamma.

OLGA and ARKADINA embrace.

Don't sell the summerhouse, Mammayinska.

ARKADINA: You mustn't speak of such things now, my sweet Olia. As the great poet Vradodsky says:

'Time enough to droop and pine
Like the turnip on the vine.
Let us rather play and sing
Like the wood-louse in the spring.'

Everyone laughs, suddenly cheered up.

DR ASTROV: Very true, dear Elena Niskova. And magnificently rendered, like the great actress you are.

OLGA: Oh yes, yes, we should have music.

DR ASTROV: You play, don't you, Trofimov? Some musical instrument or other?

TROFIMOV: Indeed. Before I was a philosophical bourgeois, I was a tutor, a student, and a strolling balladeer. I always have a balalaika somewhere about me.

He produces a balalaika.

Ah, here, you see?

ARKADINA: Do play a tune for us, dear friend. Something melancholy and atmospheric.

TROFIMOV: With pleasure.

TROFIMOV, his back to the audience, plays the balalaika as requested, as the others resume their chat.

DR ASTROV: *(With approval.)* Such a simple peasant tune.

OLGA: Yes, Doctor.

DR ASTROV: So strong and true and natural. Like the trees in the great woodlands on your estate, Madame Arkadina. The willowy birch, the birch-like willow, the delicate larch, the great oak, the lolling pine, the impetuous chestnut. I have a chart here, as it happens…

ASTROV unrolls a large, crinkly chart.

…that illustrates the precise spread of conifers and deciduous trees in this area, both native species and later arrivals, also managed woodlands and fruitful orchards, with some reference as well to the water table, major systems of natural drainage, the varieties of moss and fungi, and the density of leaf-cover down through the ages.

OLGA: 'Leaf-cover'? That reminds me, Dr Astrov. I have some raking to do in the garden. You will excuse me, Mamma, Dr Astrov, Trofimov.

TROFIMOV stops playing the balalaika.

TROFIMOV: I shall come with you.

OLGA: *(Urgently.)* No, no, Trofimov. Stay here and strum your balalaika.

TROFIMOV:	I insist, Olga Fiodorovna. I shall join you in your toil, and we can…talk. Goodbye, my friends.
ARKADINA:	Goodbye, Olgalinska. Trofimov.
	OLGA and TROFIMOV exit.
ARKADINA:	And how are you, Dr Astrov?
DR ASTROV:	As you see, Natasha Tatiana – getting older, greyer, more portly. Too much vodka and dumpling, not enough exercise.
ARKADINA:	No doubt.
DR ASTROV:	But you…you remain as beautiful as ever, Irina Nikoleyevna, and as young. Just as you were when I first beheld you. And as lovely as you were on that summer night six years ago when I gave you my heart, and you gave me…my only hope.
ARKADINA:	*(Reprovingly.)* Dr Astrov.
DR ASTROV:	*(Impetuously.)* Oh you wild dear beautiful thing, you romping raging lioness, you blazing blinding star, you…you magnificent Siberian pine! My sweet sweet Elena Avdotya Masha Arkadina…
ARKADINA:	But, Dr Astrov, what would Olga say?
DR ASTROV:	Olga?
ARKADINA:	Yes. Olga is in love with you. *(Pause.)* Didn't you know?
DR ASTROV:	*(Surprised.)* Olga? In love…with me?
ARKADINA:	Of course. Have you never looked into her eyes?
DR ASTROV:	*(Thinking back.)* Yes…last September. When she had conjunctivitis. A rather bad case. But, otherwise, no, not very often. Olga has such tiny eyes, Irina Petrovna, and they seem always to be filled with tears that course down her sallow cheeks and drip off her

pointed chin as she sobs away, winding her greasy curls around her stubby fingers. A fine girl of course, kind and pure.

ARKADINA: *(Carefully.)* But you are…not attracted to her?

DR ASTROV: No, I confess I'm not.

ARKADINA: I see. Then it is settled. Very well, Dr Astrov, I shall allow you one chaste kiss. And quickly: this may be your only chance.

DR ASTROV: A kiss! A kiss! At last! *(Afire with passion.)* Oh my dear Irina Sivnovia, my superb Eleanora Sofia Alicia Natasha Katrina Cecilia, my irresistible Anya Malensky Nikoleyevna Zanskya, my delectable …

TROFIMOV enters.

TROFIMOV: *(Interrupting everything.)* Pardon me. I wonder if I might speak to you, Madame Arkadina?

ARKADINA: *(Caught off-guard.)* … Certainly, my dear Trofimov.

TROFIMOV: Thank you. It is a rather…private matter, Astrov. You do understand.

DR ASTROV: *(Unspeakably disappointed.)* Private? But of course. You will excuse me. I think I shall stroll for a while amongst the birches and fir trees and branching junipers. *(Bowing.)* Irina Nikolayevna. Trofimov.

ARKADINA: Dr Astrov.

ASTROV exits.

Do sit down, Trofimov.

TROFIMOV: Thank you.

TROFIMOV sits. ARKADINA studies him.

ARKADINA: Ah, how you've changed, Piotr Michail Sergeyivich

TROFIMOV: Yes.

ARKADINA: Your teeth are crumbling, your complexion is poor, and your clothes are soiled. You used to be so naturally elegant, a figure of easy command and self-assurance. Now you're pathetic, even repugnant if I may say so.

TROFIMOV: Yes. I know. Olga often points it out – she's so like you in some ways. I must speak to you about her, Irina Spetsikova. I must speak to someone. I love Olga, my dear sweet girl. I adore her. I want her to be my wife.

ARKADINA: You're a fine man, Sacha Alexai Ullinoff. You have a good heart and deep feelings and an excellent grasp of social issues. But Olga doesn't love you. *(Pause.)* She loves...another in fact.

TROFIMOV: *(Upset.)* Another? I have a rival, Elena Nikolyevna?

ARKADINA: So to speak.

TROFIMOV: But who?

ARKADINA: Can't you guess? Think. *(Pause.)* Dr Astrov. She simply dotes on Astrov. Mad about him.

TROFIMOV: *(Astonished.)* Astrov?

ARKADINA: Yes, of course. Though he himself isn't at all...

TROFIMOV: *(To himself, desperately.)* Olga and Astrov! I see. I see. Of course. *(Pause. Then aloud.)* A revolver! There used to be a revolver in this dear old desk.

He opens a drawer of a desk and rummages through it.

Candles...crucifixes...playing cards... icon frames...balalaika picks...samovar strainers...

He tries another drawer and soon finds something.

TROFIMOV: Yes. Yes, here it is.

He takes out the revolver and cocks it, then puts it in his jacket pocket.

ARKADINA: My dear Piotr Sergeyivich, why in the world…?

TROFIMOV: I take my leave, Madame Arkadina. I have some work to do at last – a sacred duty, my Destiny!

As TROFIMOV is about to go, OLGA enters.

OLGA: Mamma…

TROFIMOV: *(Bitterly, to OLGA.)* Oh, Olga!

TROFIMOV exits.

ARKADINA: Such a curious fellow. And such bad teeth.

OLGA: Mamma, sweet Mamma. I have been to the dear old summerhouse… Don't sell it, Mamma. You mustn't. It's part of our lives.

ARKADINA: Don't be angry with me, Olga Ninotchka. I must sell something. I am so in debt. *(In shame.)* My dear girl, I've spent all the income from the estate.

OLGA: Oh, Mamma!

ARKADINA: I'm a silly, wasteful, extravagant woman who can't control her impulses. I give money away – hundreds of roubles – to beggars and vagrants. I give gems and jewels to wealthy people walking down the road, I don't know why. Foolish of me, I daresay. But it's my nature – please forgive me.

OLGA: *(Moved to tears.)* Oh Mamma, my dear dear Mammaskya. Forgive me. I shouldn't have spoken so to you.

ARKADINA: *(Weeping.)* Dear Olga, my sweet good daughter.

They embrace and kiss.

So we are friends again.

OLGA: Yes. Yes. *(Pause.)* Oh, I'm so unhappy, Mamma.

ARKADINA: So am I, Olganitska.

OLGA: No one knows how miserable I am.

ARKADINA: Nor how miserable I am.

Pause.

OLGA: *(Impulsively.)* Oh, Mamma, I love Dr Astrov.

ARKADINA: I know, my child. But he doesn't love you. Not in the least.

OLGA: *(Sadly.)* Yes, I know.

ARKADINA: We had quite an interesting talk on the subject not ten minutes ago. He's gone for a stroll now.

OLGA: Has he? *(She sniffs.)* And Trofimov loves me.

ARKADINA: I know, my dear girl. But you don't love him.

OLGA: Not at all, Mamma. I think he's horrid, though a very good man of course.

ARKADINA: I spoke to him just now. He seemed quite upset about something.

OLGA: *(Vaguely.)* Did he?

ARKADINA: Yes.

FIRS, frail and puffing heavily, enters on his way to the front door.

Oh, Firs!

FIRS: Yes, Mistress?

ARKADINA: Have you finished bringing in my things from the sleigh?

FIRS: Almost, Irina Nikoleyevna. Just a few more loads and I'll have it all upstairs in your room.

ARKADINA: Ah. And is old Piotr Slimovsky the driver still sitting out there in the snow?

FIRS: Yes, Mistress.

ARKADINA: *(Sympathetically.)* Well then, bring him a cup
             of tea, will you? And one of Olga's excellent
             macaroons. It's beginning to storm, I believe.

FIRS: Yes, Mistress. He'll be so grateful. Such a
             winter! Though nothing like the blizzard of
             '74, God be praised. I well remember how all
             my toes, and my fingers too…

             FIRS has gone.

ARKADINA: My little Olia, I think I shall sit here on this
             dear old sofa and you can lay your head
             on my lap and I'll stroke your flaxen hair
             as I did when you were a child. Do you
             remember?

OLGA: Oh yes, Mamma.

             *ARKADINA sits on the sofa and OLGA lays her head
             in her mother's lap.*

ARKADINA: Every year on your name-day, your dear
             Uncle Stanislav Michail Putyken Zladovsky
             would order all the peasants to gather in the
             barn and sing and dance until dawn in your
             honour. He'd hire a military band to play in
             the garden. There would be fireworks and a
             troupe of Jewish acrobats from Odessa, The
             Tumbling Ginsburgs. *(She sighs.)* I often think
             of those times as I sit by the fire on wintry
             evenings in Moscow, sipping borscht.

OLGA: *(Yearningly.)* Moscow. Moscow.

ARKADINA: Golden days, my sweet Olechna, my darling
             girl.

OLGA: *(Hopefully.)* Oh Mammaskya, I don't
             know why but I feel as though somehow
             everything will be fine again, if only we…

             A pistol-shot.

ARKADINA: *(Startled.)* What was that?

OLGA: I don't know, Mamma. Perhaps a bottle of ether exploded in Dr Astrov's medicine case.

ARKADINA: *(Relieved.)* Ah, yes.

OLGA: Or possibly there's been a duel in the neighbourhood. Or a suicide attempt. Or someone may simply have fired a revolver at someone else in a jealous fury. *(Thoughtfully.)* Indeed it did sound rather like a pistol-shot.

ARKADINA: A pistol-shot?

TROFIMOV enters, carrying a very heavily smoking revolver.

TROFIMOV: *(Panting.)* Forgive me, my friends!

OLGA: Trofimov! What are you doing with that… smoking revolver?

ARKADINA: *(Worriedly.)* Where is Dr Astrov?

TROFIMOV: *(Desperately sad.)* Oh Olga, Madame Arkadina, I'm…such a wretched failure. Just now, out in the barnyard, in a fit of jealousy for which I will never forgive myself, I shot at Dr Astrov.

OLGA: *(In horror.)* No!

TROFIMOV: And I missed him, killing instead your dear old chicken, Klubacheena.

ARKADINA: *(Shocked.)* Klubacheena?

TROFIMOV: Then, in a suicidal frenzy, I turned the weapon on myself. But in my agitation, I somehow pulled the trigger the wrong way and jammed the pistol and couldn't get it to fire! So, as you see, I live – live in disgrace and unbearable shame.

OLGA: *(Greatly concerned.)* And…and Dr Astrov?

TROFIMOV slumps silently in humiliation. ASTROV enters.

27

DR ASTROV:	Trofimov! Give me the revolver.
TROFIMOV:	Of course, Astrov.

He hands the pistol to ASTROV.

(Penitently.) Oh, my dear Astrov. Forgive me. Please forgive me, my dear fellow. It was a mad impulse of the moment. Please, my good old friend.

DR ASTROV:	*(Kindly.)* Certainly. Certainly. *(Moved.)* Here, come to my arms, Piotr Dimitri Andreyavich.
TROFIMOV:	*(Weeping.)* Oh yes, my dear Alexandrovsky Bukalloff.

They embrace, weeping.

OLGA:	Oh, Mamma. Mamma.
ARKADINA:	My dear Olga.

They embrace too, weeping.

DR ASTROV:	*(Still embracing TROFIMOV.)* Not to worry, Piotr, my dear friend.
TROFIMOV:	I deeply apologise, Doctor. Such a squalid, ugly episode. It ruins your entire visit here no doubt, and Madame Arkadina's.
DR ASTROV:	On the contrary, Trofimov. Such things serve to break up the monotony of provincial life: the stifling, endless, nerve-crushing boredom.
OLGA:	True, Doctor, nothing of interest ever happens here. *(Dreamily.)* Now, in Moscow…
TROFIMOV:	I don't entirely agree, my dear Olga Petrovna. For example, while I was stalking Dr Astrov just now in the shrubbery, a man, dressed in a grey tunic and eating radishes, galloped up to me on a splendid horse and asked me to deliver a note – this note – to you, Madame Arkadina. His name, he said,

was Ferapopopov, and I was to tell you: An auction has taken place.

TROFIMOV gives ARKADINA the note.

OLGA: An auction? Mamma!

ARKADINA: *(Opening the note.)* Let me see. *(She reads it quickly to herself. Then doomfully.)* My friends, my dear friends, it's been sold! At auction! Ferapopopov has bought it himself. 'A real bargain', he says.

OLGA: *(Mournfully.)* The summerhouse, the dear summerhouse is...gone?

ARKADINA: *(With increasing sorrow.)* The summerhouse. The garden. The barn. The stables. Olga's little school.

OLGA gasps.

The cherry orchard.

TROFIMOV gasps.

The great forest beyond.

ASTROV gasps.

(Miserably.) And this house – with all its contents: the paintings, the icons, the piano, the chandelier, the sofa, the desk, the wallpaper, the samovar.

OLGA: *(Bereft.)* Oh, Mamma!

ARKADINA: Ferapopopov says he plans to level the entire estate – to chop down the woodlands and the orchard, to pull down the great house – and to erect a huge new gas-works on the property, 'The Vladimir Ferapopopov Gas-works, serving the entire Kronosky Basin with cheap, reliable energy.'

OLGA: *(Heart-broken.)* No! No!

DR ASTROV: *(Appalled.)* My dear friends!

ARKADINA:	*(Still consulting the note.)* We are requested to 'vacate the property by 17.00 hours today. To avoid interrupting the demolition process.'
OLGA:	*(In tears again.)* Oh, Mamma.

The sound of chopping is heard.

TROFIMOV:	Listen! The chopping has begun already.
ARKADINA:	*(Grandly sad.)* I, for one, can not bear to remain here much longer, my dear ones – to stay and witness the destruction of my beloved orchard where the three seagulls used to roost, my great woodlands, my wonderful house, my dear old samovar. I must go…forever. *(She gains control of her emotions and shouts.)* Firs! Firs!

FIRS enters.

FIRS:	*(More exhausted than before.)* Yes, Mistress?
ARKADINA:	I'm leaving, Firs. Take all my things to the sleigh and prepare the horses.
FIRS:	Very well, Mistress. I may be eighty-five or ninety years old but I can still carry a few trunks and cases and chests back down the stairs and out to the sleigh again, God be praised, and harness a team of horses.
ARKADINA:	Good. *(Pause.)* And afterwards, Firs, I suggest that you take an extended holiday – spend some time with your many peasant-relations in the east.
FIRS:	*(Unable to believe his luck.)* A holiday? A holiday?
ARKADINA:	Yes. You'd better start on your journey soon. It's a long walk to Mongolia, and the roads can be treacherous this time of year.
FIRS:	God bless you, Irina Nikolayevna. I haven't had a holiday since the old Czar freed the serfs back in '61. *(Muttering happily to himself*

as he goes off.) A holiday, think of that. To see my dear mother again, and my sister, and my Uncle Vladamir Zudovsky Shubiloff…

He exits.

TROFIMOV: But Madame Arkadina, does Ferapopopov say anything else in his message?

ARKADINA: *(Looking at the note again.)* There is a postscript written in the same coarse hand. 'As I will not now be going back to Moscow, honoured lady, but staying here to supervise the work in hand, I enclose my return-ticket in the humble hope that it may be of some use to a person of your esteemed acquaintance.'

TROFIMOV: A noble gesture, the true voice of the peasant.

ARKADINA: I shall be leaving immediately – on the next available train. Would anyone wish to accompany me to Moscow?

Silence.

Anyone at all?

OLGA: *(Almost speechless with desire.)* Moscow? Go to Moscow? At last! *(Rapturously.)* Moscow!

ARKADINA: Yes.

OLGA: I should love to, Mamma. *(Pause.)* Yet I… I…

ARKADINA: You would enjoy it I'm sure, Olgavina Lubichova. And you have no reason to stay. Unless of course you and Trofimov…

OLGA: Oh no, Mamma… It's just that there is still… *(Torn by passion.)* … Dr Astrov. My dear dear Dr Astrov.

ARKADINA: *(Missing the point.)* Astrov? An interesting suggestion. Do you want to go, Astrov?

DR ASTROV:	*(Considering the idea.)* Moscow, eh? *(A pause. Then enthusiastically.)* Yes, thank you, Irina Nokolayevna. I'd very much like to. Indeed, for some time I've been thinking about moving my practice to Moscow, away from the unutterable monotony of provincial life. And now with the great forest and the orchard and this dear old house going, there's nothing at all to keep me here.
OLGA:	*(Desperately sadly.)* Dr Astrov!
DR ASTROV:	I'll go home and pack my bags in a twinkling, Irina Petrovna, and meet you at the station.
ARKADINA:	Good. We shall leave at once. *(Pause.)* But first, my dear Olga: a word.
OLGA:	Yes, Mamma?
ARKADINA:	*(Privately.)* My sweet Olgavina, my precious Olia. As you are to remain here alone, without home or family or job or income or companionship, I strongly advise you to accept Trofimov's proposal of marriage.
	Pause.
OLGA:	*(Quite defeated.)* If you think so, Mamma.
ARKADINA:	I do, my child.
OLGA:	Then, so be it. Trofimov!
TROFIMOV:	Yes, dearest Olga?
OLGA:	I will, after all, marry you.
TROFIMOV:	*(Greatly moved.)* You will? Oh, thank you, my sweet Olga. Come to my arms, my dearest, my beloved.
OLGA:	Another time perhaps, Trofimov. You may take my hand.
TROFIMOV:	Yes. Oh yes, my Olgayuska Petrovna.
	TROFIMOV takes OLGA's hand. She shudders slightly.

DR ASTROV:	A happy scene – warming the heart, as it were, against the winter soon to come. But I must go and ready myself for the great journey. Trofimov, my dear Piotr Sergeyivich, goodbye. I wish you a happy life and a splendid turnip harvest.
TROFIMOV:	*(Moved.)* Thank you, Astrov. Let me embrace you.

ASTROV and TROFIMOV embrace.

Goodbye, my dear fellow. So sorry about the attempt on your life and all that.

DR ASTROV:	Forgotten, forgotten, my old friend.

ASTROV turns to OLGA. A pause.

And now, farewell, Olga. Think well of me, my dear little Olechka Michnovia. We shall probably never meet again. I shall think of you often in Moscow, and perhaps even send you a picture postcard. 'St Basil's in the Snow' – how would that be?

OLGA:	Fine, thank you. *(Weeping.)* Goodbye, Dr Astrov, my dear dear Fiodor Orlovsky Trepliov.
DR ASTROV:	Goodbye, goodbye, dear girl. And goodbye to everyone, my dear friends, my old life, my beloved woodlands! Farewell!

ASTROV leaves, the door closes. Very soon afterwards, the jingling of his troika-bells, which fades away.

ARKADINA:	He's gone.
TROFIMOV:	He's gone.
OLGA:	*(Sadly.)* He's gone.
ARKADINA:	And now I must go. *(Sentimentally.)* Farewell dear carpet, dear icon, dear bookcases, dear old water jug, sweet youth and early adulthood and memories of bliss and vain

dreams of happiness. *(Less sentimentally.)* Goodbye, Trofimov. You are a good man, though not at all attractive.

TROFIMOV: *(Moved.)* Goodbye, my dear Irina Nikoleyevna.

ARKADINA: Olga, my dear sweet daughter, goodbye. We shall probably never meet again. Enjoy your marriage. Have many children. Be happy, my lovebirds. Joy is rare in this life: God in His wisdom has distributed it but grudgingly. Yet have hope, my dear ones, always have hope. *(To the samovar.)* Goodbye, dear samovar. *(With a sudden rush of feeling.)* Oh my dear beloved Olgavina Nazarovna!

OLGA: *(Greatly moved.)* Mamma! Darling Mammaskya!

ARKADINA and OLGA embrace, weeping and kissing again and again. At last ARKADINA steps back.

ARKADINA: But enough, my dear Olia. You know how I dislike these…emotional farewells. *(Casually.)* So I'll…just be off now, I think. *(Breaking down and weeping grandly.)* Oh, goodbye! Goodbye! Goodbye!

ARKADINA leaves, the door closes. Very soon afterwards, the jingling of her sleigh-bells, which fades away.

TROFIMOV: She's gone.

OLGA: She's gone.

TROFIMOV: And now we shall have to leave too, my beloved Olganitska.

OLGA: *(Being brave.)* Yes, Trofimov. Yes.

TROFIMOV: It will soon grow dark. Let us go to Father Zarkovsky and ask him to marry us at once. And this evening we can have your dear old chicken Klubacheena for our wedding feast.

Tomorrow, our life of poverty and toil and pain and starvation will properly begin.

OLGA: *(Making the best of the situation.)* Yes, Trofimov. Tonight we shall sleep on the bare earth of some humble hut by the swamp. And in the morning we shall join the peasants, sharing their wants and their sufferings, labouring with them for a better future. And in a hundred years from now – or a thousand – or a hundred thousand – long after we've died of starvation or overwork or diphtheria or typhus – a golden era will come, Trofimov, glorious days of happiness and beauty and peace for everyone.

Melancholy balalaika music faintly heard.

TROFIMOV: Yes, Olga, my dear Olga Lubichovna, my own sweet girl.

OLGA: Wonderful times, Trofimov. No one will remember us then of course, nor all our suffering: my frustrated love for Dr Astrov, my unhappy marriage to you, and the loss of my dear home and cherry orchard and the forests beyond. *(With bitter emphasis.)* And my never going to Moscow. But it will be worth all the sacrifice and pain and sorrow – I know it, Trofimov, somehow I know it.

TROFIMOV: Yes, yes, Olganitska Petrovna. But come, we must leave now. A new life begins, my darling, my wonderful girl.

OLGA: *(Deeply moved.)* A new life. For us and for Russia and for all mankind.

OLGA and TROFIMOV begin to walk slowly towards the door.

Oh yes. Yes. A sweet new life, my dear Pyetia Vasilly Nikolai Sergeyivivch

Alexandre Vladamir Borotski Iskanovich Yublovnik Blutinoff…

The long name fades away as they exit. The balalaika music grows louder and more heart-breaking, and the sound of chopping resumes.

Curtain.

THE LUNCHTIME OF THE GODS
Wagner's *Ring* recycled

The Lunchtime of the Gods (1994) was broadcast on BBC Radio Four. The cast was as follows:

FRAULEIN LASHMITZ, Prunella Scales
HERR HAZENBRAUER, Peter Jeffrey
ERNST, Peter Kenny

Directed by Richard Wortley

Characters

FRAULEIN LASHMITZ

HERR HAZENBRAUER

ERNST
a waiter

Darkness. We hear Wagner's 'Ride of the Valkyrie' at full strength, and we see a back-projection of Brunnhilde in horned helmet and armour, looking sternly determined. Her image slowly fades; as does the music which is replaced by the sound of a tinkling, tuneful piano, as the lights come slowly and brightly on.

Germany. An outdoor restaurant near the banks of the Rhine. HERR HAZENBRAUER and FRAULEIN LASHMITZ sit across from each other at a small table, midway through their substantial lunch. HERR HAZENBRAUER wears lederhosen and braces and, on his finger, a very formidable gold ring. FRAULEIN LASHMITZ is elegantly dressed, with a large feathered hat. After several seconds of loud, enthusiastic eating and drinking, they resume their conversation; neither speaks with a German accent. A waiter, ERNST, hovers at a distance, ever poised to be of service.

LASHMITZ:	I've never had lunch at Grossinger's before. Such excellent food, Herr Hazenbrauer. Thank you so much for asking me. And such lovely views of the River Rhine.
HAZENBRAUER:	I'm delighted you're enjoying yourself, Fraulein Lashmitz. More sauerbraten?
FRAULEIN:	*(After a pause, yielding to temptation.)* Please.

He passes a plate of it to her, she takes some.

HAZENBRAUER:	And, if I may say so, that is a most charming hat you're wearing, quite enchanting.
FRAULEIN:	Thank you. I picked it up at Schliegelmeyer and Doppelganger's on the Wotenstrasse only this morning. Especially for our meeting.
HAZENBRAUER:	Did you? And the delightful shoes?
FRAULEIN:	These? Another last-minute purchase. Zeitgeist and Umlaut's on the Flugalplatz.

HAZENBRAUER:	I'm honoured, Fraulein. More wine?
FRAULEIN:	Thank you.

HAZENBRAUER pours some wine in her glass and some in his, finishing the bottle.

HAZENBRAUER:	Ernst! Another bottle of Riesling!
ERNST:	Of course, sir. *(He exits.)*

HAZENBRAUER and FRAULEIN LASHMITZ eat and drink voraciously for several seconds. Something catches the FRAULEIN's eye.

FRAULEIN:	What a very handsome ring, Herr Hazenbrauer. Gold, isn't it?
HAZENBRAUER:	Yes. Do you like it? *(Pause.)* There's quite a story behind this little ring.
FRAULEIN:	Is there?
HAZENBRAUER:	Yes. It was made and designed many years ago, Fraulein Lashmitz, by Albrecht Nibelung himself.
FRAULEIN:	Ah. The jeweller?
HAZENBRAUER:	No, Fraulein. The goblin.
FRAULEIN:	The goblin? You do surprise me, Herr Hazenbrauer. *(Pause.)* Please go on.
HAZENBRAUER:	It's rather a long story, Fraulein.
FRAULEIN:	It sounds quite fascinating.
HAZENBRAUER:	Well, if you're sure you'd care to hear it…
FRAULEIN:	Please.
HAZENBAUER:	Very well, Fraulein Lashmitz. It's all straight-forward enough, I suppose. You see, Alberich made this ring of the very finest gold – gold which, I'm afraid, he'd stolen. From the Rhinemaidens, as it happens.
FRAULEIN:	*(Looking up from her food.)* The Rhinemaidens? *(Counting them on her fingers.)* Woglinde, Wellgunde, and… *(She thinks.)*

HAZENBRAUER: Flosshilde.

FRAULIEN: Yes, of course: Flosshilde.

HAZENBRAUER: Do you know them?

FRAULEIN: Me? No. I know _of_ them naturally. But I so seldom go near the river, Herr Hazenbrauer. On my holidays, I prefer to go climbing high in the Harz Mountains. Stout boots, a hiking song on my lips, and a flask of beer and a brockwurst-and-beetroot-sandwich on dry black bread in my little haversack.

HAZENBRAUER: Ah. Charming girls apparently, the Rhinemaidens. Good friends of Wotan, you know.

FRAUELIN: Of _Wotan_?

HAZENBRAUER: The Chief of the Gods, yes.

FRAULEIN: _(Impressed.)_ Fancy! Friends of Wotan.

HAZENBRAUER: And he got the ring from Alberich, and took it immediately to Fafner and Fasolt.

FRAULEIN: The auctioneers?

HAZENBRAUER: No, no. The giants.

FRAUELEIN: _(Feeling a fool.)_ The giants, of course. But why, Herr Hazenbrauer? – considering that it was, so to speak, the property of the Rhinemaidens.

HAZENBRAUER: As ransom, I'm afraid, Fraulein Lashmitz. _(He eats.)_ Delicious pig-trotters. Such a tangy jelly.

FRAULEIN: _(Eating and agreeing.)_ Mmn. Piquant yet somehow unctuous. _(She has a bit more.)_ But...ransom, you say, Herr Hazenbrauer. Ransom for whom?

HAZENBRAUER: For Freia.

FRAULEIN: Freia? The goddess of youth and beauty, is she not?

| HAZENBRAUER: | Quite. A very attractive creature, apparently. Though, if I may say so, not as lovely as you, Fraulein Lashmitz. I doubt that even she has your sea-blue eyes, firm lank limbs, pert nostrils and swirling golden hair. |
| FRAULEIN: | *(Modestly.)* Thank you, Herr Hazenbrauer. *(With appreciation.)* Lovely plums in sauerkraut. |

They eat enthusiastically for several seconds.

	But didn't Fafner and Fasolt eventually have a bit of a…falling-out?
HAZENBRAUER:	Yes indeed, and over this very ring. Fafner slew Fasolt in fact, a great family scandal at the time.
FRAULEIN:	Yes, I think I remember.
HAZENBRAUER:	And afterwards, to make matters worse, Fafner took the ring away with him and hid in a cave and – in order to guard it most effectively – he transformed himself into a dragon.
FRAULEIN:	You astonish me, Herr Hazenbrauer. What a world we live in.

ERNST enters with a bottle of wine on a tray.

| ERNST: | The wine, sir. |
| HAZENBRAUER: | Ah. |

ERNST uncorks the wine and, after HAZENBRAUER waves him away, he exits.

	More Riesling, Fraulein Lashmitz?
FRAULEIN:	Just a little. To wash down all the Weiner Schnitzel and black sausage and liver dumplings.
HAZENBRAUER:	Of course.

He pours a glass for her, then one for him. He takes a sip, then resumes his account.

Now, Wotan was most fearfully upset, furious even.

FRAULEIN: At Fafner, you mean? For taking the ring?

HAZENBRAUER: Yes. *(Dramatically.)* He feared that all this conflict could lead to the destruction of Valhalla itself.

FRAULEIN: Valhalla? The Abode of the Gods?

HAZENBRAUER: Precisely. In Wotan's view, there was only one thing to do if he wished to forestall the approaching calamity. He must – and with all possible haste – seduce Erda, the goddess of wisdom (no easy task I can tell you), and thus beget the Valkyries. And so he did.

FRAULEIN: The Valkyries, Herr Hazenbrauer?

HAZENBRAUER: *(With deep appreciation.)* Superb wild maidens, Fraulein Lashmitz, huge and hugely erotic, wearing magnificent metal corsets and breastplates like the shield of Achilles – arms like oaks, elbows like mountain peaks, riding through the air on wingéd steeds.

FRAULEIN: Ah.

HAZENBRAUER: A lovely sight. Especially on fine summer evenings with pink clouds and the streaming rays of the setting sun behind them. A picture, Fraulein Lashmitz.

FRAULEIN: Mmn.

HAZENBRAUER: Grimgerde, Waltraute, Schwertleite: lovely names for lovely ladies. And Brunnhilde: so beautiful, so loud, shaming the very thunder with her bellowing shouts.

FRAULEIN: But how did the ring come into your possession, Herr Hazenbrauer?

HAZENBRAUER:	Be patient, be patient, my dear Fraulein Lashmitz. *(He sips some wine.)* Now, one day, when Wotan was…

ERNST has arrived.

ERNST:	Pardon me, sir. Will there be anything else?
HAZENBRAUER:	Yes please, Ernst. Some more asparagus, I think. And two portions of your bowel of pork in savoury grease (one of the house specialities, Fraulein Lashmitz; you have no idea). A few dry Bavarian sausages. And more wine: a bottle of Liebfraumilch and one of Zeitgumpster.
ERNST:	Thank you, sir.

Exit ERNST.

HAZENBRAUER:	To continue, Fraulein. Wotan was going to Valhalla one day when he was met along the way by Donner, Froh and Fricka.
FRAULEIN:	His three dogs?
HAZENBRAUER:	Hardly, Fraulein. Two gods and one goddess. As he crossed the bridge to Valhalla, Wotan heard, from the deepest depths of the Rhine far below, the gurgling voices of the Rhinemaidens.
FRAULEIN:	Waglinde, Wellgunde, and…
HAZENBRAUER:	Flosshilde.
FRAULEIN:	Ah, yes.
HAZENBRAUER:	They were pleading, you see, with Wotan to restore to them the ring. But in vain, as you know, for he had recently given the ring to the giants, Fafner and Fasolt.
FRAULEIN:	True, very true. Rather a dilemma for him, Herr Hazenbrauer.
HAZENBRAUER:	Quite. Now, some time later, after Wotan had begotten Siegmund and Sieglinde…

46

FRAULEIN: The Walsung twins?

HAZENBRAUER: Yes. A delightful pair – golden-curled, rose-lipped – and so devoted to each other. *(He smiles at the thought.)* And, after *they* had in turn begotten Siegfried…

FRAULEIN: *(Shocked)* Begotten? The Walsung twins… had *begotten*? On each other? I like to think of myself as broadminded, Herr Hazenbrauer, but this…this is… *(She searches for the words.)*

HAZENBRAUER: Another family scandal, I fear, Fraulein. And to make matters worse, Sieglinde was married at the time – to Hunding. Now, as luck would have it, Wotan's daughter Fricka was the goddess in charge of marriage, and she was of course most distressed.

FRAULEIN: I should think so.

HAZENBRAUER: She insisted that Wotan must punish Siegmund and Sieglinde, and he at last agreed.

FRAULEIN: Well, I'm very pleased to hear it, Herr Hazenbrauer.

HAZENBRAUER: Brunnhilde, on the other hand, ever the soft-hearted girl, strove to protect the Walsung twins – in defiance of Wotan's command – and so she was put to sleep by Wotan, albeit reluctantly. And to ensure privacy for his daughter, he placed a circular wall of flame around her rocky couch.

FRAULEIN: It must have been quite stifling. A wall of flame, you say – and she in all that heavy armour.

HAZENBRAUER: Well, Fraulein, the offspring of Siegmund and Sieglinde was Siegfried – a good friend of mine by the way – and a lovely fellow: generous, very brave, very blond, a fine singer (a tenor in fact). I often accompany him on the glockenspiel. We do Prussian folk ballads, gipsy serenades, sometimes even little songs of my own composition.

FRAULEIN: *Do* you?

HAZENBRAUER: *(Modestly.)* Yes. Now, one day, Siegfried went to Fafner's.

FRAULEIN: Fafner's. The kosher delicatessen on the Rupertplatz?

HAZENBRAUER: The giant, Fraulein.

FRAULEIN: Oh, of course.

HAZENBRAUER: Though at this particular point, the *dragon* – as he now was. You *will* recall…

FRAULEIN: The dragon, yes, yes, yes.

ERNST enters with a tray of food and wine.

HAZENBRAUER: Seigfried then slew Fafner and took the ring. – A very messy business apparently – blood and dragon-slime and eyes and scales and internal organs everywhere.

ERNST: Your bowels in grease, sir.

FRAULEIN: *(With relish.)* Thank you, Ernst.

ERNST places the food and drink on the table, then HAZENBRAUER waves him away, and he goes. The FRAULEIN tucks in.

HAZENBRAUER: Afterwards, it was merely a matter for Siegfried to stride through the ring of flame that surrounded the vast and slumbering form of Brunnhilde, her bosom heaving (as Siegfried never tires of recounting) 'like the raging sea in a fire-storm'. And although Brunnhilde was, in truth, three or four times his age – and weight – and was attired in the least flattering of ensembles (helmet, visor, chainmail) – the older woman in short, if looking rather more like the older man – Siegfried fell in love with her instantly

48

and awakened her with a fervent kiss.
Whereupon they were betrothed on the spot.

FRAULEIN: Such a romantic first meeting, Herr
Hazenbrauer.

HAZENBRAUER: Yes. And they have been inseparable ever
since, the very image of the contented
couple, however unconventional. And that,
Fraulein Lashmitz, is the story of my ring.

FRAULEIN: I see. What a fascinating history it has; really
I should never have guessed. And such a
happy ending too.

HAZENBRAUER: Yes. Shall we drink to the loving couple,
Fraulein Lashmitz?

FRAULEIN: But certainly, Herr Hazenbrauer.

They raise their wine glasses.

HAZENBRAUER: To Brunnhilde and Siegfried. Long life and
years of untroubled joy and incessant bliss.

FRAULEIN: Brunnhilde and Siegfried.

*They touch glasses and drink. HAZENBRAUER then
turns his full attention to the food.*

HAZENBRAUER: Might I…trouble you for the mustard,
Fraulein?

FRAULEIN: Of course.

She passes him the mustard.

HAZENBRAUER: Thank you.

FRAULEIN: But…the ring, Herr Hazenbrauer. Why is it
now in your possession?

HAZENBRAUER: It's not exactly mine, Fraulein Lashmitz; it's
on loan. Siegfried is a close friend, as I say,
a great chum in fact (and so is 'Brunie' of
course – Brunnhilde, that is). I told Siegfried
I had an engagement this afternoon with a
lady of great beauty, a mysterious woman
of the world I'd just met, and he pressed

the ring on me, he absolutely insisted – so
I would look my best, you know. Indeed,
Fraulein, I'm wearing his lederhosen too.
You see?

He rises from the table to give her a better look.

FRAULEIN: Magnificent, Herr Hazenbrauer.

HAZENBRAUER: Shall I…spin round?

FRAULEIN: Please.

He does.

(She sighs in admiration.) Are the braces really
studded with…?

HAZENBRAUER: Dragon's teeth, yes. A lovely touch that. And
look, these are Siegfried's private stockings
too – with the Walsung family crest.

He shows them off, then sits.

FRAULEIN: A most impressive display, Herr
Hazenbrauer. Thank you.

HAZENBRAUER: Not at all, my dear Fraulein Lashmitz. My
adorable Fraulein Lashmitz.

FRAULEIN: *(Modestly.)* Herr Hazenbrauer.

HAZENBRAUER: Call me…Dort. And you, you are…

FRAULEIN: I? …Gerd.

HAZENBRAUER: Gerd. Good. More wine?

FRAULEIN: Yes please.

*He fills both their glasses. The FRAULEIN takes a great
gulp, but HAZENBRAUER swirls his thoughtfully.*

HAZENBRAUER: *(In expansive mood.)* Ah, what a very
memorable afternoon this has been for me,
Gerd. Superb food and drink, a glorious
view of the Rhine, and an incomparable
companion at my table.

FRAULEIN: It's very kind of you to say so…Dort. But I fear that I and my little world must seem rather drab to you.

HAZENBRAUER: *(Resuming his eating and drinking.)* No, no, Gerd.

FRAULEIN: You move in such glamorous circles, Dort. Your good friend is Siegfried, a hero and the grandson of a god no less. Indeed, you sit there now, wearing his heroic lederhosen and braces and ancestral stockings – and his magnificent ring with all its romantic associations, glittering away on your finger. *(Pause.)* Dort, I… Oh, you'll think it absurd of me I know, but I wonder… *(She pauses again.)*

HAZENBRAUER: Yes, Gerd? What is it?

FRAULEIN: I wonder, my dear Dort, if perhaps I might… if I might try on the ring – just for a moment.

HAZENBRAUER suddenly stops eating.

I should love to see how it looks on me. A great gold ring like that, on my pale, slender, unworthy finger. A ridiculous fancy I suppose, but…

HAZENBRAUER: My dear Fraulein Lashmitz, I'm so sorry. I'm afraid such a thing is out of the question. I do apologise.

FRAULEIN: But Dort, I should be so pleased and so honoured. To wear, however briefly, a ring of such distinction, and such powerful allure. An allure not unlike your own, my dear dear Dort.

HAZENBRAUER: Fraulein, you must forgive me, but it is quite impossible.

FRAULEIN: *(Fondly.)* Dort, my Dort, my darling Dort, if you let me wear the ring, then – directly after lunch – you may accompany me to my little chalet deep deep in the bird-resounding linden tree forest, a lamp of light in the green darkness. There we shall go to my perfumed bedchamber where you will encounter a wilderness of excruciating pleasures, my Dort, a universe of secret delights, fleshly ecstasies – gross, exquisite, maddening.

HAZENBRAUER: I'm most frightfully sorry, Fraulein, but I fear that I simply can't. It must seem very rude of me, I know. Do let me explain. It is a matter of Honour, Fraulein Lashmitz. You see, I swore to Siegfried that I wouldn't remove this ring from my finger until I return it at last to him. He plans to give it to Brunnhilde as a sort of wedding present. Rather than be false to my vow to Siegfried, I would happily fling myself off a Carpathian peak, or into the reckless waters of the Rhine, or (as in the present circumstances) deny myself the undoubted pleasures of your intimate favour. *(Pause.)* More bowels, Fraulein?

FRAULEIN: So your answer is no.

HAZENBRAUER: Alas, it is.

FRAULEIN: In that case, Herr Hazenbrauer, I must make an announcement. I'm afraid I've been less than candid with you about who I am. Indeed, I am not Fraulein Lashmitz, a strangely attractive unmarried woman from Düsseldorf.

HAZENBRAUER: You're not?

FRAULEIN: It was but a ruse to gain your confidence and, in time, your ring. *(Pause.)* I am, in fact, Flosshilde.

HAZENBRAUER: *(Very surprised.)* Flosshilde? One of the Rhinemaidens? Sister to Woglinde and Wellgunde?

FRAULEIN: Quite so, Herr Hazenbrauer.

HAZENBRAUER:	*(Observing her carefully.)* So…you have feet then? I mean: rather than fins or flippers.
FRAULEIN:	I am not a walrus, Herr Hazenbrauer. My sisters and I are supernatural sea-creatures with the lineaments of ordinary mortals, though possessing extraordinary powers both physical and prophetic.
HAZENBRAUER:	Of course.
FRAULEIN:	We seldom stray from our watery path-ways – Woglinde, Wellgunde and I. Most of our time, Herr Hazenbrauer, is passed languishing on the sea floor, or sporting with billows in the sparkling sunshine, or guarding our inestimable treasures in secret places amongst the deep rocks or in oozy sea-caves. Which brings me to my purpose. I have, Herr Hazenbrauer, emerged from my river today on a very special mission: to retrieve from you that ring, fashioned from gold sifted from the salt-streams of my beloved Rhine – Rheingold in fact – and therefore the exclusive property of my sisters and myself.
HAZENBRAUER:	I see. So, had I let you wear the ring …
FRAULEIN:	I should, of course, have slipped it on my finger, run to the banks of the Rhine, executed a perfect dive into its waters (my native element), and dissolved from human sight. And as I pierced the surface, the river gods would have sounded their echoing horns to welcome my return. Such a charming custom.
HAZENBRAUER:	Ah.
FRAULEIN:	And yet now that you know who I really am, you will no doubt consider it your duty as a gentleman and a man of honour to return

	my ring to me. *(Pause.)* The ring please, Herr Hazenbrauer.
HAZENBRAUER:	Alas, I am afraid, Fraulein Flosshilde, that I must remain true to the vow I made Siegfried.
FRAULEIN:	Was Wotan true to his vow to return the ring to us? Was Sieglinde true to her marriage vow to Hunding? Was Kierbroten true to his vow to the Schnockerel Brothers of Westphalia?
HAZENBRAUER:	*(With finality.)* I am sorry.
FRAULEIN:	*(With a sigh of exasperation.)* Very well, Herr Hazenbrauer. You force me to exercise my supernatural physical powers. If you do not remove the ring from your finger, I have no choice but to remove your finger – and then, from it, the ring.
HAZENBRAUER:	*(Appalled.)* Fraulein!
FRAULEIN:	I shall simply snap your finger off your hand and the ring will be mine.
HAZENBRAUER:	Fraulein!
FRAULEIN:	I warn you, my dear Herr Hazenbrauer. I can do it as easily as I can break this dry Bavarian sausage. You see?

She takes up a Bavarian sausage from the table and lightly tries to break it, but fails to do so.

(Vexed.) Himmel!

She tries again with greater effort and at greater length, twisting and wrenching it about, but without effect. She sighs, and puts the sausage aside.

(Disappointedly.) Clearly my remarkable physical powers are on the wane. I should have known of course. Whenever I'm out of the water for an extended period, my great strength tends to drain away.

HAZENBRAUER: *(With relief.)* So it would seem, Fraulein. The ring will remain with me, and with Siegfried. I think our lunch has ended. After the pudding and coffee of course. *(Firmly.)* There will be no more talk of the ring.

FRAULEIN: On the contrary, Herr Hazenbrauer. My only hope now is to tell you the rest of the story of the ring, the part you didn't tell me.

HAZENBRAUER: The *rest* of the story? Is there more?

FRAULEIN: Yes, of course: that which is yet to happen. My prophetic powers are, I believe, as yet undiminished. As you will discover, Herr Hazenbrauer, the ring will inevitably come to me, whatever you decide to do; if not now, then after much pain and travail.

HAZENBRAUER: Indeed?

ERNST glides towards the table.

FRAULEIN: Yes. You see, Herr Hazenbrauer, if you fail to…

ERNST: Pardon me, madam. Will there be anything else? Pudding perhaps?

FRAULEIN: Yes, thank you. A Black Forest gâteau please. And on the side, a sacher torte, Emperor's schwarren, gugelhupf with almonds and a dozen spitzbuben.

HAZENBRAUER: The same for me, Ernst. Custard on the gugelhupf please.

ERNST: Of course, sir.

He exits.

HAZENBRAUER: You were saying, Fraulein Flosshilde…?

FRAULEIN: Herr Hazenbrauer, if you return the ring to your friend Siegfried, he will indeed give it to Brunnhilde, and then he will set out on a series of adventures.

HAZENBRAUER:	Such is his firm intention, I believe.
FRAULEIN:	*(Darkly.)* But all the time, the Norns have been busy, Herr Hazenbrauer.
HAZENBRAUER:	The Norns?
FRAULEIN:	The three grey sisters of fate.
HAZENBRAUER:	*(Never having heard of them.)* Of course. The Norns.
FRAULEIN:	Always spinning, spinning, spinning their skein of life – which breaks!
HAZENBRAUER:	*(Alarmed.)* I see.
FRAULEIN:	Brunnhilde will give Grane to Siegfried.
HAZENBRAUER:	Grane?
FRAULEIN:	Her horse.
HAZENBRAUER:	Ah, yes.
FRAULEIN:	Now, Herr Hazenbrauer, somewhere along the Rhine, not terribly far from here in fact, live the Gibichungs.
HAZENBRAUER:	The Gibichungs? Yes: Gunther, Hagen, and their sister Gutrune. A peculiar family. They keep themselves very much to themselves, I believe.
FRAULEIN:	And yet, in the near future they will welcome Siegfried into their castle, Herr Hazenbrauer. And as they do so, they will cunningly administer to him a love-potion in a drinking horn. And Siegfried, all unknowing, will drink and fall deeply in love with his hostess Gutrune, and quite forget his bride, the incomparable Brunnhilde.
HAZENBRAUER:	*(Incredulous.)* Siegfried? Forget Brunnhilde?
FRAULEIN:	It seems unlikely I know, Herr Hazenbrauer. But life can be very strange, stranger even than the wildest piece of fiction.
HAZENBRAUER:	I suppose so, Fraulein.

FRAULEIN: Now mad with love, Siegfried will ask to marry Gutrune. Her brothers, Hagen and Gunther, will agree, but only if Siegfried will help Gunther marry Brunnhilde with whom he has long been in love.

HAZENBRAUER: Oh!

FRAULEIN: Hagen will suggest to Siegfried that, for this purpose, he will require the use of Tarn.

HAZENBRAUER: Tarn? Another horse?

FRAULEIN: No.

HAZENBRAUER: A cow?

FRAULEIN: No, Herr Hazenbrauer, a helmet. A helmet whose wearer can assume any appearance he desires – man, woman, fish, fowl, frog, flea, pillar of mist, fruit salad – according to preference.

HAZENBRAUER: Astonishing.

FRAULEIN: And so Gunther requires Siegfried, love-crazed by the potion, to go to Brunnhilde (once more ensconced in her ring of flame) and carry her to him, to Gunther, as his bride.

HAZENBRAUER: *(Enraged.)* The very idea! Quite disgraceful!

FRAULEIN: Well might you say so, Herr Hazenbrauer. Ah, the puddings!

ERNST has entered with a vast tray of puddings. He lays them on the table and exits. HAZENBRAUER tucks in.

So one day, Siegfried – Tarn (his helmet) on his head, his sword (Notung) in his hand, his boots (Viergemund and Viergelunde) on his feet – sets out to capture Brunnhilde and bring her back to wed Gunther.

HAZENBRAUER: *(Eating.)* Worse and worse, Fraulein Flosshilde.

FRAULEIN:	At dusk, he comes upon Brunnhilde and, in the guise of Gunther, seizes her and takes the ring – *that* ring – *my* ring – from her finger and brings her, helpless and distraught and massively wriggling, to the Gibichungs' castle.
HAZENBRAUER:	Utterly appalling!
FRAULEIN:	Another spitzbuben?
HAZENBRAUER:	Please!

She offers a plate of them, he takes a few.

FRAULEIN:	When they arrive, Siegfried gives Brunnhilde to Gunther and claims Gutrune for his bride.

The FRAULEIN eats.

A great double-wedding is arranged: Siegfried is to wed Gutrune; Gunther, Brunnhilde. The table is set, the food is prepared, the guests have arrived, the musicians are tuning up, the presents are stacked in the great hall. But just before the ceremony begins, Brunnhilde happens to hear Gunther call Siegfried 'Siegfried', and she sees the ring on Siegfried's finger and recognises him.

HAZENBRAUER:	*(Apprehensively.)* Oh! Oh!
FRAULEIN:	There is the most terrible row, Herr Hazenbrauer. Brunnhilde, never a woman to hide her feelings, becomes tremendously indignant, and rages and shouts and shrieks and bellows – and, I'm afraid, conspires with Hagen to kill the unfortunate Siegfried, himself innocent of all sin.
HAZENBRAUER:	No! No!
FRAULEIN:	A hunt is arranged, and during the course of it, my dear Herr Hazenbrauer, Hagen spears Siegfried, who dies in voluptuous agony.

HAZENBRAUER: Siegfried! No! Oh, no!

ERNST arrives with another laden tray.

ERNST: Coffee?

FRAULEIN: Thank you so much, Ernst.

ERNST sets down the coffee things and exits. The FRAULEIN pours a cup for HAZENBRAUER and for herself.

Brunnhilde, at last informed – by my sisters and myself, by the way – of the love-potion and its unfortunate effects and of the blameless conduct of her late husband, is filled with fury and curses the gods of Valhalla and orders a colossal funeral pyre to be erected. Siegfried is piled upon it, and Brunnhilde, after taking the ring from his finger, sets him alight and withdraws. Then she mounts Grane…

HAZENBRAUER: …the horse…

FRAULEIN: …and spectacularly gallops at full speed into the flames – and perishes.

HAZENBRAUER: Oh! Brunie!

FRAULEIN: *(Sipping coffee.)* What follows next, Herr Hazenbrauer, is only to be expected in the circumstances. The River Rhine overflows; we Rhinemaidens, riding the surf, pluck the ring from the flaming finger of Brunnhilde, now sadly sizzling on the pyre; my two sisters – Woglinde and Wellgunde – drown Hagen; and I flourish the ring triumphantly in the bright and smoky air, at last and forever in our possession.

HAZENBRAUER: *(Overwhelmed.)* I see.

FRAULEIN: A dramatic moment of course, and one to cherish. And yet, Herr Hazenbrauer, it will also prove to be (one might say) the twilight of the gods. Valhalla, blighted by Brunnhilde's curses and the effects of evil, will now itself be in flames. The great era of Wotan will have passed. And that…is the end of *my* story.

HAZENBRAUER: *(Quite taken aback)* … Yes.

FRAULEIN: And all this will happen, Herr Hazenbrauer, if you don't give me the ring now.

HAZENBRAUER: I…I…

FRAULEIN: A heavy responsibility. All the deceit, strife, treachery, heartbreak, murder, sacrifice – the deaths of Siegfried and Brunnhilde (your dear 'Brunie'). Not to mention the fall of Valhalla, the departure of the gods, the confounding of destiny itself. And in the end, as you see, I shall have the ring anyway.

She sips her coffee.

So, what is your answer now, Herr Hazenbrauer?

A long, thoughtful pause.

HAZENBRAUER: *(Shaken and wavering)* A very powerful argument, Fraulein Flosshilde. I don't know… *(Pause.)* A tragic story of course. No man of feeling could fail to be moved by the prospect of such terrible events. *(Another pause.)* But Fraulein, you must understand. I have made a vow to Siegfried. If what you say is to be his fate – why, the man is a hero of immortal fame; he will embrace it. It even has a sort of epic grandeur to it, like a tale of ancient times. Yes, I shall keep the ring.

FRAULEIN: *(With a great sigh.)* Very well, Herr Hazenbrauer. So be it. I'm too weak to continue any longer. *(She sips her coffee.)* Excellent coffee.

HAZENBRAUER: I hope all this won't inconvenience you greatly, Fraulein.

FRAULEIN: I confess it won't be easy for us Rhinemaidens in the years ahead. We are, after all, part of the old tradition, Herr Hazenbrauer. We'll have no place in the coming era, I fear.

HAZENBRAUER: No, Fraulein Flosshilde?

FRAULEIN: No. You see, after Valhalla vanishes, entirely new belief-systems will emerge and take over the world.

HAZENBRAUER: I see. What sort of 'new belief systems' precisely? Can you foretell that?

FRAULEIN: Oh yes. In this general geographical area, Christianity mainly.

HAZENBRAUER: *(A new word for him.)* Christi-anity?

FRAULEIN: Mmn. A doctrine of love and sin, Herr Hazenbrauer. *(Sips coffee.)* It will bring centuries of inquisitions, crusades, European wars: oppression, repression, depression. A few positive contributions as well of course: Christmas pudding, mince pies, hot-cross buns, chocolate eggs – and some highly attractive architecture, particularly cathedrals. Nothing to compare with Valhalla of course.

HAZENBRAUER: *(Rather guiltily.)* I see, Fraulein.

FRAULEIN: Everything will be forgotten, and everyone: the gods, the giants, the goblins, the Valkyries, your beloved Siegfried, his beloved Brunnhilde, even we Rhinemaidens will disappear from the world's memory, or at best become merely the stuff of myth and a very well-known music-drama.

HAZENBRAUER: *(With interest.)* A music-drama, Fraulein Flosshilde?

FRAULEIN:	Yes, an enormously long one, I believe, Herr Hazenbrauer, to be written in the late nineteenth century.
HAZENBRAUER:	Ah. I'm a bit of a composer myself, you know. You couldn't hum a few bars from it, could you? Or perhaps even whistle a little tune or two?
FRAULEIN:	I can do better than hum or whistle, Herr Hazenbrauer. Feeble though my powers are, I think I can summon up a bit of enchantment.

She reaches into her handbag, and removes two conch-shells.

Here, take these conch-shells.

She hands them to HAZENBRAUER.

Now hold one against each ear, pressing them firmly to get the full effect.

He does so.

All right?

HAZENBRAUER:	Yes.
FRAULEIN:	Quite ready?
HAZENBRAUER:	*(Nodding yes.)* Mmn.

The FRAULEIN gestures mystically at the shells. Suddenly we – and HAZENBRAUER – hear ten seconds or so from Wagner's 'Siegfried': Siegfried and Brunnhilde singing hard. It grows ever louder, but breaks off when HAZENBRAUER takes the shells from his ears.

(In some shock.) Whatever was that, Fraulein Flosshilde?

FRAULEIN:	Siegfried and Brunnhilde. The love duet I believe.

HAZENBRAUER puts the shells to his ears again; there is another, briefer blast.

(*Dismissively.*) It doesn't sound a bit like them. *(With distaste.)* And the music itself, Fraulein…

FRAULEIN: And yet it will be the source of their immortal world-wide fame, Herr Hazenbrauer. That particular passage comes from somewhere near the middle of the second or third day of the performance, if I'm not mistaken.

HAZENBRAUER: Indeed? I see. *(A lengthy pause. Then, with some reluctance.)* Very well, Fraulein, I agree. You may have the ring. It is yours.

FRAULEIN: The ring? The ring! *(Simply delighted.)* Oh, thank you so much, my dear Herr Hazenbrauer. But – if I may ask – why?

HAZENBRAUER: I am, Fraulein Flosshilde, very fond of music. Call me old-fashioned if you will, but I love a good tune, a sweet clear line of melody. And I will not be responsible for such… gross disharmonies as I've just heard, such ghastly blasts of sound, repulsive in the extreme. And to think, Fraulein, this is how my Siegfried and my Brunnhilde would be forever remembered. Why, they would become the objects of mockery and ridicule wherever this 'music-drama' was played. Siegfried will understand my decision, I know. The man is a musician himself. *(Fondly.)* You should hear him sing 'The Jolly Milkman', one of my own ditties.

FRAULEIN: *(Urgently.)* Then swiftly: the ring, Herr Hazenbrauer! Take off the ring and give it to me!

HAZENBRAUER: Of course, Fraulein, immediately. I'm so sorry.

He tries to remove the ring. It won't budge. He tries again, but in vain.

I don't seem to be able to get it off.

FRAULEIN: What?

HAZENBRAUER: I've eaten so much this afternoon that I appear to have swollen up considerably, particularly my fingers. One moment.

He tries again, unsuccessfully. He pauses and sighs.

FRAULEIN: Let me help.

She leans across the table and pulls energetically at the ring as HAZENBRAUER pulls in the opposite direction. No luck.

Here, smear your finger with some of the grease from the bowel of pork.

HAZENBRAUER: Yes, of course. Most resourceful.

He slops the grease generously on his finger.

Now pull, pull, pull, my dear Fraulein!

Much pulling back and forth from them both, much grunting and sighing and panting too, especially from the FRAULEIN, a great communal effort; the contents of the table rattle and clatter and clink.

I think it might be coming.

More pulling, no success.

Possibly not. Just one more good pull perhaps, Fraulein.

FRAULEIN: *(Exhausted by the activity.)* No, no, I can't, Herr Hazenbrauer. I'm growing weaker and weaker.

She releases her grip, though HAZENBRAUER is still trying.

(Lightly gasping.) I really should go. I must return to the Rhine, you see.

HAZENBRAUER stops pulling.

HAZENBRAUER: But no, Fraulein. Surely you won't go into the water now, so soon after eating. You'll get dreadful cramp.

FRAULEIN: There are some things far worse than cramp, Herr Hazenbrauer. If I don't return to the river at once, I fear that I shall grow faint, and then fall to the floor, gasping and flopping about like a flounder drowning in air. And, at last, expire – there, on the restaurant carpet.

HAZENBRAUER: *(Sadly.)* Fraulein Flosshilde!

FRAULEIN: *(Gasping.)* Yes. I must rush to the banks of the River Rhine and leap in immediately. Goodbye, Herr Hazenbrauer. *(To the ring.)* And, dear ring, auf wiedersehen.

HAZENBRAUER: *(Regretfully.)* Goodbye, Fraulein Flosshilde. I should have given you the ring earlier, before the pudding.

FRAULEIN: Would that you had, would that you had, Herr Hazenbrauer. Still, thank you for an excellent lunch. I shall long remember it. Take my hat, will you?

He nods, and she gives him her hat.

And now, do excuse me. If you wish to follow my progress to the river, listen in on the shells.

She gestures towards the shells as before.

Farewell again.

She rises slowly from her chair, and staggers feebly from the restaurant. HAZENBRAUER presses the shells to his ears. We hear the FRAULEIN breathing heavily, her feet padding for several seconds to the river's edge. A pause, then her voice.

I come, I come, my sisters.

We hear the splash of a perfect dive, and the sound of the river gods' horns welcoming her home. A pause. HERR HAZENBRAUER removes the shells from his ears and sits in silence. After a while, ERNST comes to the table.

ERNST: Has madam gone, sir?

A long pause.

HAZENBRAUER: *(Miserably.)* Yes.

ERNST: Can I bring you anything else, sir?

HAZENBRAUER: The bill please.

ERNST: Of course, sir.

He starts to go.

HAZENBRAUER: And... *(Pause.)* ...some rhubarb strudel.

ERNST starts to go again.

With cream.

ERNST: Thank you, sir.

ERNST exits. A long pause.

HAZENBRAUER: *(Guiltily.)* What have I done?

Darkness slowly falls, though a light remains shining on HERR HAZENBRAUER, and the sound of 'The Ride of the Valkyries' can be faintly heard.

(Despairingly, his hand clutching his brow.) Oh great Wotan, what have I done?

The music is louder now, and rising.

Curtain.

THE BARDS OF BROMLEY

a comedy

The Bards of Bromley (2004) was broadcast on BBC Radio Four. The cast was as follows:

MRS. SWERDLOW, Julia McKenzie

WILLIAM WORDSWORTH, Timothy West

GEORGE ELIOT, Amanda Root

AUGUST STRINDBERG, Paul Rhys

A A MILNE, John Moffatt

JOHANN WOLFGANG VON GOETHE, John Rowe

DOCTOR, Philip Fox

Directed by David Hunter

Characters

MRS SWERDLOW

WILLIAM WORDSWORTH

GEORGE ELIOT

AUGUST STRINDBERG

A A MILNE

JOHANN WOLFGANG VON GOETHE

DOCTOR

A college lecture-room in Bromley, Kent.

The room is dimly lit, with several staggered chairs facing the lecturer's desk. A A MILNE, a genial middle-aged man, sits at the head of the class, drawing on his pipe. At the very back sits JOHANN WOLFGANG VON GOETHE, severe of aspect, enveloped in what seems to be a cloak. GEORGE ELIOT, a woman in her late thirties, enters and heads for the chair furthest from the front, but, finding it occupied, settles for another nearby. A man with a trim beard and carrying a black case enters; he pauses, looks round and, as if having realised his mistake, promptly exits. As he does so, MRS SWERDLOW, a woman in her fifties (spectacles dangling from a long cord round her neck), enters; she flips on a wall-switch lighting up the room, then sits at the lecturer's desk piling it with papers. WILLIAM WORDSWORTH, clean-shaven and slightly dishevelled, comes in and takes a seat near the front. He is followed by AUGUST STRINDBERG, sharply dressed and with a natty moustache, who sits behind him. Each of them, we now see, has brought along a large collection of manuscripts. MRS SWERDLOW is glancing through her stack of papers as MILNE turns to WORDSWORTH.

MILNE: *(Softly.)* First time? At the college.

WORDSWORTH: *(Rustic accent.)* Ay.

MILNE: It's my second course here. I did 'Mongolian Country Cooking' last term. Very informative. Remarkable what they can do with a musk-ox and a few vegetables. Quite an eye-opener. *(Pause.)* You're not originally from round here, I take it.

WORDSWORTH shakes his head.

Nor am I. Though I feel quite at home in Bromley now, 'gone native' as they say. And everyone is so friendly. It's almost like a village, and yet just ten minutes or so from Croydon. *(Pause.)* Interesting chap at the back, wearing a cloak. So wise-looking somehow. A foreigner, don't you think?

WORDSWORTH looks round at last.

WORDSWORTH: *(Disapprovingly.)* Ay.

MILNE: May I introduce myself? I am…

MRS SWERDLOW rises to address the group, interrupting MILNE.

MRS SWERDLOW: Good afternoon, gentlemen, and welcome. When we announced our intention of starting a writers' workshop here at West Bromley College, we little expected to receive so many manuscripts of such high quality. I am Jacqueline Swerdlow, and it has been my arduous duty to select the five outstanding examples, and my great pleasure to invite you, their authors, here today. Over the past few years, in similar workshops I have conducted throughout the country, I have been privileged to discover and develop several promising new writers who have gone on to make their mark. Regina Bloxham whose book of poetry, *Daisies on My Ceiling*, has recently been published by the Regina Bloxham Press; Norris Grudgeon's play, *Dead for a Ducket*, was performed last year at the Old Sulphur Pit, Dagenham; and Simon Jayston's romantic novel, *Five Lords-a-Loving*, comes out in the autumn, all being well. And who can say, gentlemen, if in time some of your names will rank with theirs? At any rate I hope everyone will have a creative and rewarding experience.

MILNE: Speaking for us all, Mrs Swerdlow, I'm quite certain we will.

SWERDLOW:	*(Grateful for the response.)* Thank you so much. And talking of books, my latest – *Write On!: 114 Easy Steps to Literary Success*, third edition, personally autographed by myself, published by the St Ubalda Press, Merthyr Tydfil, £18.99, ten percent reduction on the first five copies sold – is available after the workshop, or indeed any time during it.
MILNE:	*(With interest.)* Is it? Excellent.
SWERDLOW:	Well, now that we have the formalities out of the way, let me remind you that the efforts represented here today cover a wide range of literary disciplines, so we can expect a most stimulating first session. Each of you has, I trust, received copies of everyone else's work so we may discuss them together – offering encouragement and support, sharing impressions and suggestions.

A slight murmur of unease from the group.

I think we're all here, so I shall call the roll.

She flips through her papers, finds at last what she wants, and begins to read.

Mr…William…Wordsworth.

WORDSWORTH:	Ay, Mrs. Over here.
SWERDLOW:	Good afternoon, Mr Wordsworth. *(To the others.)* As you all know, Mr Wordsworth has tried his hand at writing a little poem about clouds and lambs and flowers and such – in his native Derbyshire I believe.
WORDSWORTH:	Lake District, Mrs.
SWERDLOW:	The Lake District of course. And we'll be dealing with his 'Daffodils' shortly – a poem which displays, if I may say so, a certain sentimental, even anthropomorphic view of nature perhaps.

WORDSWORTH: Ay?

SWERDLOW: *(Over-riding WORDSWORTH's response)* But to continue. *(Back to her papers.)* Mr…George Eliot. *(Pause.)* Mr Eliot? *(She looks about.)* Are you here, Mr Eliot?

GEORGE ELIOT: Present.

SWERDLOW: *(Surprised to find GEORGE ELIOT so lady-like)* Oh. *(Recovering.)* Welcome, Mr Eliot. And what a very attractive ensemble. *(To the others.)* George is a budding writer of fiction, and he has just written a novel, a rather lengthy one which I hope all of you had the fortitude to plough through, called *Middlemarch*. Though I'm bound to say that *Mid-March* would be rather more grammatically pleasing, don't you think? Or perhaps *The Ides of March* – that has a certain literary thrust behind it. Just a thought, Mr Eliot.

ELIOT: But…

SWERDLOW: We'll return to you later. *(Back to the roll.)* Mr August…Strindberg.

STRINDBERG: *(Fiercely, and with a slight Swedish accent.)* Yes!

SWERDLOW: *(Startled by his ferocity.)* Hello. Mr Strindberg's play, *The Dance of Death*, is a rather quirky piece I think you'll agree…

STRINDBERG: *(Fiercely again.)* Quirky?

SWERDLOW: And such a morbid title too. Not likely to attract the passing trade on Shaftsbury Avenue. Perhaps we should try something more frothy and light-hearted. *Happily Never After* – or *Mid-Wife Crisis* – or *Swede and Sour*. Leave it with me; I'll have a think. For the moment, let us go on. *(She consults the roll.)* Mr A A Milne.

MILNE: *(Mildly.)* Here I am. Good afternoon, Mrs
               Swerdlow.

SWERDLOW: Good afternoon, Mr Milne. As you'll all
               recall, Mr Milne's little story of bears and
               pigs and kangaroos offers a rare glimpse into
               the natural world of our native woodlands –

               Sussex I believe.

MILNE: Quite so. *(To the others.)* Delighted to be here,
               everyone.

SWERDLOW: There is also an intriguing view of an inter-
               species relationship – an erotic bond perhaps
               – between a bird and a bear.

MILNE: A bird, Mrs Swerdlow?

SWERDLOW: Yes. The robin, Christopher.

MILNE: Oh. A slight misunderstanding here I think.
               Christopher Robin is a boy.

SWERDLOW: A boy?

MILNE: My son, in fact. A lovely little chap.

SWERDLOW: *(With growing interest.)* Fascinating. More
               of this later. *(The roll again.)* And last,
               a man who has written novels, poetry,
               plays, philosophical treatises and scientific
               speculations – Jack-of-all-trades and master
               of none – Johann Wolfgang von Goethe. Is
               that you, Mr Goethe? In the black, swirling,
               writer's cloak?

GOETHE: *(Lugubriously.)* Ja!

SWERDLOW: Good. Mr Goethe, of course, has submitted
               a work called *Faust*, in two huge volumes, all
               written in his own tiny and distinctive hand,
               a real challenge.

               GOETHE grunts enigmatically.

SWERDLOW: But let us now begin, let us open ourselves
               to the creative process. As Hamlet says
               somewhere, 'On your imaginary forces

work.' *(Pause.)* First, Mr Wordsworth and his little poem.

WORDSWORTH: Ay, very well.

WORDSWORTH rises from his chair, and goes and stands before the group. Then, with his customary relish, he recites.

'I wandered lonely as a cloud
That floats on high o'er vales and hills,
When all at once'…

SWERDLOW: *(Interrupting.)* No need for that, Mr Wordsworth. We've all read your piece I think. Well, my first problem with it – before I open the discussion out to everyone else – is…the style.

WORDSWORTH: The style, Mrs?

SWERDLOW: It's very…*jingly*, isn't it, Mr Wordsworth? – so sing-songy.

(Sing-songily.) 'I *wan*dered *lone*ly *as* a *cloud*

Ti-*tum*, ti-*tum*, ti-*tum*, ti-*tum*,

Ti-*tum*, ti-*tum*, ti-*tum*, ti-*tum*,

Ti-*tum*, ti-*tum*…

You must break up the rhythm, man:

'I wandered lonely like I was some sort of *(Pause.)*

Cloud, floating round and round here and there in the *(Pause.)*

Sky.'

Stretch the line, *shatter* the line, fragment it, destroy it!

WORDSWORTH: But…

SWERDLOW: And all those rhymes… Really, the way you write, Mr Wordsworth, it's as though Modernism had never happened.

WORDSWORTH: *(Unfamiliar with the term.)* As though what?

SWERDLOW: *(Pained to point it out.)* And there's the archaic vocabulary. 'Oft when on my couch I lie…' – '*Oft*'? My dear Mr Wordsworth, how frequently do you say, 'Oft'?

Pause.

WORDSWORTH: Oft. Full oft. 'Tis the way one talks, the way everyone talks. 'Tis part of my method, you see.

Lapsing into blank verse.

I speak but with the common tongue of men.
No formal language, nor the eloquence
Of mind-seducing speech more suitable
To lofty pulpit or the laurelled stage,
To high debate or grove of academe.
But simple truth serene, simply expressed,
Whereby each humble man may understand.
As when the zephyr in a field of corn –
Bright grain of Ceres – rustleth all the sheaves
Unnoticed, so will my plain utterance bring –
Passing with ease into the reader's mind –
The deep philosophy of daily things.

Pause.

SWERDLOW: *(Not understanding at all.)* … Sorry?

MILNE: I think I understand. You're saying, if I'm not mistaken, Mr Wordsworth, that you wish to use the every-day language of ordinary speech.

WORDSWORTH: Forsooth, it is my mission and my pride.

MILNE: An admirable object, sir. Well done, well done indeed.

SWERDLOW: Yes, yes, quite. And indeed there are some things about Mr Wordsworth's poem that I like very much. For example the lines: 'A poet could not but be gay / In such a jocund company.' Truly revealing.

WORDSWORTH: Is it?

SWERDLOW: The image of the poet who could not but be gay consorting with the fluttering, dancing, indeed thrusting daffodils. You should bring out this element more frequently, Mr Wordsworth. (Or 'more oft', as you would say.) An intriguing subtext.

WORDSWORTH: *(Another new word.)* 'Subtext'?

SWERDLOW: *(To the group.)* And now, what is your view of the poem? Mr Eliot?

ELIOT: A very pleasant little thing. But if I may say so, I'm not certain that mere poetry is the proper medium for great ideas. Perhaps instead a novel on the subject would be rather more satisfactory.

WORDSWORTH: A novel? About daffodils?

ELIOT: Not entirely, of course. As things develop, nasturtiums and begonias for example might be introduced into the plot, together with selected mosses. *(Envisaging it.)* Yes, a huge novel, charged with philosophy and social history, touching on the plight of the poor, the obligations of wealth, the nature of the affections, the ethics of Spinoza, and the reform of the divorce laws. I myself should certainly read it – with enthusiasm and perhaps a little envy.

SWERDLOW: A challenging notion, Mr Eliot. And now, Mr Milne, tell us please: Do Mr Wordsworth's daffodils bloom for you?

MILNE: *(Enthusiastically.)* I think his poem is absolutely topping. Loved the dancing flowers, loved the floating cloud. 'That inward eye/Which is the bliss of solitude' – a lovely phrase, and so true. It reminds me of a holiday I took a few years ago – a long weekend really – in Hazelbyrne, just outside

Wrexham. (Do you know it?) Daffodils everywhere dancing about, giving their all, inexhaustible plucky little things. And the waves of the lake, bowing and curtseying in time to the gentle tide. Butterflies on every bloom, the dew still hanging on the rhubarb. The 'peep-peep-peep' of the linnet, the 'hummm' of the bluebottle, the swish of the trout frolicking happily in every stream, filling the heart with joy and the eyes (not infrequently) with grateful tears. It was all as Mr Wordsworth describes it and feels it; indeed his art is nature itself. Wonderful work, sir. My congratulations.

(MILNE rises and shakes WORDSWORTH's hand.)

WORDSWORTH: *(Taking it as his due.)* Thank you, Milne.

SWERDLOW: And now, Mr Goethe, your views.

GOETHE: *(Firmly.)* Nein!

SWERDLOW: *(Surprised.)* Pardon, Mr Goethe?

GOETHE: Nein. *(Pause.)* Nein!

SWERDLOW: I see. Very well. Then, Mr Strindberg, have you any reflections on the poem?

STRINDBERG: Indeed I have. My dear Wordsworth, please consider: Your beloved daffodils, far from being blameless ornaments of nature, are the tumours of the earth – vile excrescences rising unbidden, posturing like prostitutes, flaunting their bodies, sending their stink abroad, luring the callow bees into their rank entrails. All flowers – daffodils, the noxious buttercup, the sinister periwinkle – are nourished by rotting corpses and the worms that feed on them, blind and voracious gluttons, grubs and slugs and things of slime. *And* the working classes – they play their part in it somehow, I assure you.

MILNE:	Steady on there, old fellow. Surely buttercups have much to recommend them. Why, one day Christopher Robin was…
STRINDBERG:	Ignore it if you will, Wordsworth, but daffodils, like all plants, are a plague and a parasite on man, sprouting and festering in the cracks and corners of life. I would kill all flowers – raze them like invading troops. And trees as well. What are they but gigantic weeds, giving shelter and succour to birds with their idiotic cries and filthy personal habits? No, death to all vegetation, all verdure, all foliage, all growth. Give me honest sterility, the dead promise of a barren field.
WORDSWORTH:	A bleak and horrible doctrine, Strindberg.
STRINDBERG:	Embrace the bleakness in life, man. Court the horror. Only then will freedom come, the freedom of disgust!
SWERDLOW:	Mr Strindberg's point is perhaps too powerfully put. But has it never occurred to you, Mr Wordsworth, that Nature may simply not be your proper subject? There is so much more to write about in life – the world of sport, high fashion, the royal family. Mr Strindberg's views may seem…
WORDSWORTH:	Strindberg's views are those of a deranged Swedish blackguard.
STRINDBERG:	*(Into his stride.)* And as for wandering 'lonely as a cloud' – my play *The Dance of Death* is about <u>true</u> loneliness, the loneliness of a man surrounded by family and friends. And there is loneliness in my *Miss Julie, The Ghost Sonata* and *The Dream Play*. Did you steal the theme of loneliness from me? It seems an extraordinary coincidence.

WORDSWORTH: I steal from your abominable plays? A preposterous accusation. Why I've been wandering lonely as a cloud for years, all over Cumbria. And Somerset. Ask anyone.

ELIOT: *(Suddenly remembering.)* And Yorkshire too, I believe. Of course! I thought you looked familiar, Mr Wordsworth. A few summers ago when I was up at Haworth visiting my friends the Brontë girls – Annie, Emmy and dear little Lottie – I regularly saw a wild-eyed dishevelled man in distressed corduroy, accompanied by a pinched-faced lady in a scarf, striding across meadows, scrambling up cliffs, wading through thorn and bracken on the dismal moors…

WORDSWORTH: Ay, that would have been my sister and I – 'wandering lonely as a cloud' we were, Mr Eliot.

ELIOT: Once or twice I saw you simply standing, staring blankly at the sky.

WORDSWORTH: Reflecting in tranquillity, most likely.

ELIOT: I see. I'm afraid that, when I first arrived, I took you for country beggars, and even gave you each sixpence.

WORDSWORTH: *(The memory still fresh.)* Tuppence, actually.

ELIOT: Was it?

STRINDBERG: *(With derision.)* 'Lonely as a cloud.' 'Lonely as a cloud'? What a ridiculous conceit. A cloud is not lonely. It is also not happy, or indignant, or easily embarrassed, or secretly amused. A cloud is a phenomenon of nature – and is therefore wicked, malevolent, cunning, a curse on man and an engine thwarting his every design.

WORDSWORTH: I will not hear Nature so vilely abused. Nature has all the innocence of a child –

she is bliss, she is inspiration, she is the emblem of the infinite soul. We're talking about rainbows here, of sunsets and star-clad nights and bright mornings filled with echoing birdsong. *(He turns to the others for support.)* Why, who among us has not at some time followed a cloud for the better part of a day, striding after it through bogs and misty meadows, golden valleys and dank woodlands, barren heaths and waving fields of borage to fall at last on the dewy grass, foot-sore and heart-enriched? *(There are no replies either way.)* The new-born infant lists joyfully to secret instructions from the warbling bird, the bleating lamb, the buzzing fly; the very winds whisper wisdom to his attentive soul, wisdom alas forgotten by corrupted and corrupting men.

STRINDBERG: This is mere prissiness, Wordsworth – swooning like a girl at dewdrops, gasping at the passing clouds, treasuring the philosophy of drooling babies. While all the time the snake Life lays her black eggs in your spleen, gnawing on your vitals, gorging on your blood, slurping up your bile…

SWERDLOW: *(Urgently.)* I think this might be a good time for a little tea break. We'll resume the workshop in a few minutes. This way please, gentlemen.

They disperse to a long table upstage, which, as we see when MRS SWERDLOW whisks off the covering cloth, is laid, rather lavishly, for tea. MRS SWERDLOW and GOETHE, as it happens, pair off, as do WORDSWORTH and MILNE, and STRINDBERG and ELIOT. Eating and drinking ensue. As each couple speaks, the others will mime their conversations.

SWERDLOW: An Eccles cake, Mr Goethe?

GOETHE:	*(Forcefully.)* Nein, danke!
SWERDLOW:	Ah.
	Pause.
MILNE:	Tea, Mr Wordsworth?
WORDSWORTH:	Yes, thank you, Milne.
MILNE:	Milk?
WORDSWORTH:	Please.

MILNE pours it.

WORDSWORTH: *(With approval.)* Fresh country milk.
(Then, reciting.)
'For lo! The udder yields its lactic tide
Abundant, from the bovine underside.'
Some lines of my own. From 'Reflections on
Seeing a Cow Being Milked in a Pasture Just
Outside Keswick in Early Autumn'.

MILNE: *(Pouring the tea.)* Ah. Very gripping. Sugar?

WORDSWORTH: Thank you. Seven lumps please.

MILNE drops in the lumps.

My sister usually prepares my tea. A
wonderful woman, 'a violet by a mossy
stone'.

MILNE: Is she?

WORDSWORTH: Oh, yes. Attentive, sympathetic, an
inspiration. An excellent cook, a talented
beekeeper, a brilliant floral arranger, a
committed diarist, and a devoted nurse to the
sick. Back in Grasmere, my slightest fever or
physical discomfort would send her rushing
across meadow and moorland, even in the
face of lashing storms, to gather medicinal
herbs from remote mountain tops. Such a
sensible creature. Are you a married man,
Milne? *(Remembering.)* Oh, of course you are:
that little son of yours…Craig, was it?

MILNE: I think you mean Christopher. Yes, I am.

WORDSWORTH: Dorothy isn't really free anyway. She and Coleridge (my friend) have an understanding. A misunderstanding in my view. *(He studies the tea offerings. Then, with pleasure.)* Ah look, Windermere bilberry loaf.

MILNE: So it is. Lovely.

They each take a slice, and then, nibbling and sipping, drift downstage.

WORDSWORTH: Such a dull crowd here today. To be frank, Milne, I dislike the company of writers – vacant, vain, citified sots. A group of publishers – yes of course, that could be a truly rewarding experience. A roomful of starving country beggars – certainly, they always have an enormous fund of wisdom to impart, easily transmuted into blank verse. A grove of ancient trees – they express their own deep philosophy to those who will look and listen and feel. But writers… *(He sighs.)*

MILNE: In that case, I wonder that you've come here today, Mr Wordsworth.

WORDSWORTH: I am an unregarded, unpublished genius, Milne. My agent insisted I attend in the hope of making myself 'marketable' – much against my own wishes I may say, and those of my beloved sister.

MILNE: Who are you with?

WORDSWORTH: My agent? Louise Bouffant of Sheldrake and Muldive in Ullswater. And you?

MILNE: Sidney Kravetnik. He's at Ashvail, Mastodon and Quezmore. I used to be with Neil Runcible of Ridgeway, Bland and Futon on Regent Street, a lovely man, absolutely topping, but such a pessimist.

WORDSWORTH: So is Louise. Mind you, I can see her point. No one these days seems all that bothered about sheep and trees and clouds, never mind the lesser celandine. 'Tis very sad.

MILNE: I greatly admired your 'Daffodils' poem. Have you written many others?

WORDSWORTH: Hundreds of odes. Over a thousand sonnets on ecclesiastical and geographical subjects alone.

MILNE: I see. Strindberg was very tactless about your poem I thought.

WORDSWORTH: Did you? I agree. *(With repugnance.)* I cannot abide Swedes. …I speak, of course, of the people not the root vegetable. Indeed, I composed a sequence of poems in praise of root vegetables only last spring. If you're interested, I think I can remember most of them.

MILNE: Truly? I'd be honoured. Such a…boldly original choice of subject.

WORDSWORTH adopts a recitation pose, and clears his throat grandly.

WORDSWORTH: 'Behold it splendid in the distant field, Yon solitary Turnip! Eve and morn, In shade of night and golden height of noon'…

His voice fades away, though he continues to mime and MILNE to listen, as we now eavesdrop on STRINDBERG and ELIOT, deep in chat.

STRINDBERG: So your agent advised you to come here too?

ELIOT: Yes, Mr Strindberg.

STRINDBERG: Who are you with, Mr Eliot?

ELIOT: Noorish and Keppleman of Bristol. And you?

STRINDBERG: *(Very Swedishly.)* Hasseltrad and Spoondenfjord of Uppsala.

(He sips some tea.) Tell me, what did you think of my play?

ELIOT: Very powerful, Mr Strindberg. It was like dwelling in someone else's nightmare – a madman's perhaps. Full of horrible moments and terrible scenes. Tremendously upsetting.

STRINDBERG: *(Pleased.)* Too kind.

ELIOT: More tea?

STRINDBERG: No, thank you. Well, Mr Eliot, I must say I admired your novel. Strong, masculine, bold, forceful, forthright and coldly logical.

ELIOT: *(Delighted and very relieved.)* Did you really think so? Thank you so much for those generous words. To be frank, Mr Strindberg, I hadn't shown *Middlemarch* to anyone at all before. It's been my great secret.

STRINDBERG: Has it indeed?

Pause.

ELIOT: *(In reflective mood.)* When I was a child, <u>all</u> my writing was secret. Father was a strict Evangelical, you see, and strongly disapproved of fiction. I had to hide from him all the manuscripts of my three-volume novels – sometimes in my toy-box, sometimes in my dolly cupboard. Denied pen and ink, I would scribble away on whatever poor paper I could find with one of Mother's darning needles dipped in strawberry jam – seedless for preference. A messy business.

STRINDBERG: *(Sympathetically.)* My dear fellow.

ELIOT: But I was found out, Mr Strindberg, betrayed by a trusted nanny. As a result, when I was five I was sent away to boarding school, to curb my wild spirit. Yet even there I secretly continued to write, exposing – in one of my novels of the period – the network of bullying and exploitation that is at the core of the infant playground, and its relationship to the struggle between Capital and Labour in the wider world.

STRINDBERG: I see. Remarkable.

ELIOT: In more recent times, of course, I've been far more open about my novels, though sadly no publisher has as yet shown any interest in them – *Adam Bede*, *The Mill on the Floss*, *Silas Marner* – and *Shep, a Poodle of the Plains* (a rare departure into the realm of canine fiction). Yet *Middlemarch* seems so ambitious an undertaking…great themes, many characters and such complexities of plot – I've often doubted that I was quite equal to the task. The very thought has often reduced me to tears. But now – to have received such encouragement from a man like you… I'm most grateful, Mr Strindberg.

STRINDBERG: Do call me 'August'. Like the English month.

ELIOT: Thank you, I shall.

STRINDBERG: And, like the English month, I have my bright periods as well as my occasional thundery showers. Moments of wild ecstasy and violent rage, sudden fainting fits, days of crippling doubt, months of arrogant certainty – I've known them all. *(Pause.)* And I hope I may be permitted to call you 'George'.

ELIOT: *(Impulsively.)* I'd rather you call me…'Mary Ann Evans'.

STRINDBERG: Would you? It seems rather a liberty. Unless… *(Realising at last.)* You mean to say that you are a woman?

ELIOT: *(Whispering.)* Yes.

STRINDBERG: Of course. That explains so many things: your voice, your clothes, your sausage-curls – not to mention your prominent matronly bosom. *(Fondly remembering.)* You know, for a while I thought of calling myself 'Leticia' –

'Leticia Beauregard-Samuels of 15 The Chase, Merton'. I don't know why. Just a sudden urge that came over me, that sprang out of my guts, out of the seething sod of my bowels, out of the sweaty coils of my secret pulsating innards. You know the feeling.

ELIOT: 'George Eliot' is my *nom de plume.* It's so no one will know I'm a woman. Women, you see, are often underestimated as writers. You *will* keep my secret.

STRINDBERG: Not a word, I promise you. My dear Mary Anne Evans, shall we drink a toast to our new friendship? I have a flask here of my favourite Swedish schnapps – Frupelstrood, a speciality of the Upper Transrandabander region.

He produces the flask.

Pure as rage, bitter as sorrow, harsh as fate, sudden as revenge. Here, I'll fill your teacup.

He pours some into ELIOT's cup.

ELIOT: I think not, August, but thank you.

STRINDBERG: No? I shall, if I may.

He gulps it down instantly.

Marvellous. But have a little swallow, my dear. Please do. In my country – and indeed, out of my country – it is considered a great insult to the Swedish nation and to our glorious ancestors if such an offer is declined.

ELIOT: Is it?

STRINDBERG:	Come, we shall toast your achievement – your *Middlemarch*.
ELIOT:	Well, in that case, just a drop.
STRINDBERG:	Good.
	He fills a cup and half-fills another.
	To *Middlemarch*.
ELIOT:	To *Middlemarch*.
	They both drink. ELIOT gasps loudly.
	(Barely able to speak.) Lovely.
STRINDBERG:	Are you married, Mary Ann?
ELIOT:	*(Still recovering from the drink.)* No.
STRINDBERG:	Excellent. So you have eschewed the marriage knot. The marriage *noose*, strangling desire, murdering impulse. Nor am I married – now.
ELIOT:	I do live with a man however, a Mr Lewes. *(Pause.)* In sin, as it happens.
STRINDBERG:	Do you?
ELIOT:	Not *much* sin, to be honest. Lewes is a good man, but in truth we never exchange intimate familiarities. Greetings in the morning – yes of course, handshakes upon retiring, affectionate glances at birthdays, passionate discussions of social issues, but nothing more. It is our way you see, or at least *his* way.
STRINDBERG:	Yet a fine woman like you with a superb mind and such beguiling sausage curls – some men would find you irresistible. Genius allied with intelligence and allure – what more could one desire?
ELIOT:	*(Very pleased.)* 'Genius, intelligence and *allure*'? But Mr Strindberg…August… In

truth, I…I've never been counted among the beauties…

STRINDBERG: Ruggedly beautiful, I should say, Miss Evans. Like Mt Zortstroom, its craggy bulk rising out of the swirling Nordic mist. But tell me. Have you ever been to my country? – to Sweden? *(He pronounces 'Sweden' in swooping Scandinavian syllables.)*

ELIOT: I'm afraid not. I've seldom been out of England in fact. I've seen much of Warwickshire, and I know Coventry very well, especially the area round the lending library and the old butter market. My life has been somewhat circumscribed I suppose.

STRINDBERG: But have you never yearned to see the fjords at sunrise? To feel the icy hand of the north wind as it shifts the great snowdrifts beneath the steely, brightening sky?

ELIOT: I've been rather more interested in the living conditions of the farm-workers in the Midlands – their children's want of education, the women's bitter struggle against deprivation and oppression.

STRINDBERG: Women and children and farm-workers? But the fjords offer a real lesson in life! And seen with me, standing at the prow of my ship, 'The Kugglefryer', as it prances through the wintry gales, the ice clinging to your ears, your skin cracking with the cold and the cracks stinging in the salt breeze, drenched to the bone, shuddering with discomfort and howling with pain as you face down the roaring elements…! *(He sighs, invigorated by the thought.)*

ELIOT: *(Thrilled.)* The way you put it of course, it sounds very tempting.

STRINDBERG: *Be* tempted, my dear Mary Ann. Come with me to Sweden. Now.

ELIOT: I couldn't, August. I haven't the required knitwear. And then there's Mr Lewes.

STRINDBERG: At least meet me tomorrow to talk it over. Or to say, 'Farewell forever'. The Bromley Arms on the High Road. I'm always there for lunch on Thursdays, they do cottage pie. A chat, nothing more. I shall tell you about my homeland, of the ice floes and the treacherous millrace, and of the great spring thaw, for you have thawed my heart, Mary Ann; my bitter winter is past, the sunlight of your gaze has released me – like a glacier I float free down the open path of my destiny. Be with me, my blazing midnight sun, never to set. Warm this fond heart, melt these adoring eyes into tears. You shall be my muse and I yours. I ask nothing more, my incomparable Mary Ann.

ELIOT: *(Distinctly tempted.)* Oh, August!

STRINDBERG: More Frupelstrood?

ELIOT: Yes please.

STRINDBERG recharges the teacups and they drink, exchanging knowing glances. But we return to WORDSWORTH and MILNE.

WORDSWORTH: *(Finishing up a poem.)*

…'In our own lives, whate'er we do or say,
To woe confined or wandering passion's way,
Full many a lesson can we learn from thee,
Thou humble radish, rooted and yet free.'

MILNE: Excellent. *(He applauds briefly.)* Thank you so much, Mr Wordsworth. Your poems on root vegetables are absolutely riveting. Were they published, I feel sure they would cause a sensation. *(Pause.)* Care for more tea?

As WORDSWORTH considers the question, STRINDBERG and ELIOT slowly exit, hand in hand.

WORDSWORTH: No thank you, Milne.

He draws a small vial from his inside jacket pocket.

But perhaps you'd like a bit of this.

MILNE: What is it?

WORDSWORTH: I'm not certain. A tincture I believe. Something Coleridge gave me to try. It's a kind of mild relaxant. He says he can't praise it too highly. 'Honey dew' is how he describes it. 'The milk of Paradise'. Good for diarrhoea apparently.

MILNE: None for me thank you, Mr Wordsworth. I'm fine.

WORDSWORTH: I think I may have a drop. Life is so difficult when the world seems almost wilfully blind to one's greatness. Everything reminds me of my failure, Milne, particularly this workshop. *(Pause. Then tenderly.)* And yet, you know, I once wrote, 'All that we behold/ Is full of blessing.'

MILNE: An inspiring sentiment, Mr Wordsworth.

WORDSWORTH: I had such plans, Milne. I was to speak for the common man, and to him. But the common man proved to be so…common, without any interest at all in my poetic effusions. *(He sighs.)* Yes, a touch of the tincture perhaps.

WORDSWORTH swallows a drop or two.

We're with MRS SWERDLOW and GOETHE again.

SWERDLOW: Then possibly some Black Forest gâteaux, Mr Goethe?

GOETHE: Nein, danke.

SWERDLOW: No? *(She checks her wrist-watch.)* Well, I suppose after all it's time for us to resume. *(She looks about; then, more loudly.)* Is everyone here? Where is Mr Strindberg? And Mr Eliot?

MILNE: They strolled outdoors a minute or so ago, Mrs Swerdlow. 'To gaze at the sun setting behind the Bromley hills,' I believe they said. Hand in hand, as I recall.

SWERDLOW: Did they? Mr Eliot is such an eccentric young man. Mr Strindberg is strange too, in his way.

WORDSWORTH: Strindberg is a toxic monster, like a great spider or a scorpion – a Swedish scorpion. If my sister Dorothy were here, she would write something very rude indeed about him in her diary.

SWERDLOW: Still, he is an intriguing figure, Mr Wordsworth, and rather…romantic.

WORDSWORTH: *(A bit wildly, the laudanum beginning to take effect.)* Romantic? Strindberg? With his carefully tousled hair and waxed moustache? *I*, Mrs Swerdlow, *I* am romantic – a creature of impulse like a summer butterfly or a cloud animated by the breeze, friend of the moon, brother of the raindrop, cousin of the waterfall, son-in-law of the thunderbolt! *(Ardently.)* Why, back in Grasmere I was in regular converse with wild flowers, welcoming blossoms of every hue to our dear meadow – thistlewort, lady's smock, John-on-his-pillow, St Anne's cuticle, the greater bladderflax, the lesser spleenbane – and every spring I was the proud host of golden daffodils. And I was even a romantic young revolutionary once, pledged to every rebellion going, thirsting for worldwide freedom and the fall of princes and privilege. Though I confess I've adjusted my views somewhat since then. *(Rather embarrassed.)* Indeed I've written a dozen sonnets in support of the death penalty, and one or two which favour the arrest and public flogging of all visiting Frenchmen – as a warning to them, and for the innocent pleasure of passers-by. And yet, in my youth, I fell passionately in love with a young French woman, and even got her with child. *(Moved.)* Dear Annette, standing in the morning light, with her soft smile and the baguette under her arm. 'Earth,' as I remarked at the time, 'hath not anything to show more fair.' *(With a sigh.)* Bliss was it in that dawn to be alive, quite frankly. *(Pause.)* You know, Milne, I think I may try another drop of Coleridge's tincture. Are you certain you won't join me?

MILNE: Thank you no, Mr Wordsworth. I'm quite happy with my tea and scone. And I'm very fond of this honey, most exceptional.

WORDSWORTH: *(Yawning.)* As you please.

He has a swallow.

SWERDLOW: Well, I daresay we can give the others a few more minutes. You were saying, Mr Goethe?

GOETHE stares at her in stony silence.

WORDSWORTH: *(Seizing the opportunity.)* 'Verses on Various Agricultural Implements'.

He strikes a pose.

'Lo,
The hoe!...'

MILNE: *(With relief.)* Ah, but here they are!

ELIOT and STRINDBERG enter gaily chatting, ELIOT patting her hair, STRINDBERG adjusting his tie.

SWERDLOW: Mr Eliot, Mr Strindberg – we're reconvening the workshop.

STRINDBERG: *(Softly.)* Now you sit here, my dear, by me.

ELIOT: *(Softly.)* Forever, August. Do keep hold of my hand.

STRINDBERG: Of course. For without it, Mary Ann, I fear I should soon become quite lost in this great world.

ELIOT: *(Sighing fondly.)* Oh, August.

STRINDBERG: And on a finger of that sweet hand of yours I shall soon, if I may, place a ring – my mother's ring.

ELIOT: Will you?

STRINDBERG: It was given her by my father on the day of their betrothal. Sadly, he took it back from her years later when he discovered that she had been false to him – with Anderson, the Danish blue cheese-monger. He also removed the tip of her nose, slit it off with a penknife – the traditional Swedish punishment for such a transgression. The ring, with its cluster of rubies and pale sapphires, I've kept on my mantelpiece for many years. I also have the nose somewhere, in a little pink box. It turns up from time to time.

ELIOT: What a romantic story, August. He must have loved her very much.

STRINDBERG: We Strindbergs do *everything* very much, my dear, as you will see.

SWERDLOW: In your places too please, Mr Goethe, Mr Wordsworth, Mr Milne.

They settle in, WORDSWORTH and MILNE near each other, as are ELIOT and STRINDBERG. MRS SWERDLOW riffles through her papers.

Now we come to Mr Eliot's novel, *Middlemarch*.

ELIOT: Yes, Mrs Swerdlow.

SWERDLOW: Well, this needn't detain us long. It is clearly the work of an amateur, though one of some promise. A few tips. More confusion in your narrative would be welcome, Mr Eliot. Make the reader work a little. Who ever said fiction is fun? No, it is labour – often long, bitter, unrewarding labour.

ELIOT: Is it?

SWERDLOW: And when your characters speak, they should, I feel, swear a good deal more, especially your low, vile, agricultural workers. Foul language in their mouths is as natural to them as the muck on their boots or the filth beneath their fingernails.

ELIOT: *(Offended.)* Mrs Swerdlow…

SWERDLOW: Don't worry. I've marked places in the text where such things can be easily inserted, and compiled an alphabetical list of appropriate terms, which I hope you'll find useful

She brandishes a sheaf of papers, which she gives to ELIOT.

Oaths, expletives, obscenities, curses and blasphemies gleaned from my wanderings in rural Surrey, chiefly on the outskirts of Greater Dorking. The Bricklayer's Arms was a particularly fruitful source. *(Pause.)* And now, Mr Wordsworth, what are your views of Mr Eliot's novel?

WORDSWORTH: *(Somewhat drowsily.)* Well, Mrs, I should say that it's rather too long to begin with. It should be brief, succinct and, preferably, in blank verse, concentrating on the story of a country lad – a youth of great promise and simple innocence, who goes to the city and loses his way amongst the bright lights and temptations of Bromley. While back in his native hills, his poor parents…

Overcome by the laudanum, he yawns and instantly falls asleep, lightly snoring.

STRINDBERG: Precisely.

SWERDLOW: Mr Wordsworth?

WORDSWORTH snores on, more loudly.

(Distinctly peeved.) Perhaps later. Mr Goethe, your observations on *Middlemarch* please?

Pause.

GOETHE: Nein!

SWERDLOW: I see. Mr Milne?

MILNE: It is a superb work, I think, absolutely topping. So wise and mature, especially from a beardless youth like Mr Eliot, with his little piping voice.

ELIOT: *(Trying to lower her voice.)* Thank you.

MILNE: Tremendously promising. Loved the style, loved the narrative, loved the characters. A triumph, dear fellow. My warmest congratulations.

ELIOT: *(Low voice again.)* Thank you again.

SWERDLOW: Now, Mr Strindberg, have you any thoughts?

STRINDBERG: Yes. *(Pause.) Middlemarch* <u>is</u> a remarkable novel, indeed quite the worst I have ever read or ever hope to read.

ELIOT: *(Shocked.)* August!

STRINDBERG: Meretricious, presumptuous, false and everywhere strident. Its female characters, bluestockings and harpies, its male characters utterly unconvincing. The philosophy shallow, the style inane, the plot overblown, the politics malicious and meddling!

ELIOT: *(Deeply hurt.)* No, August!…

STRINDBERG: A long and ghastly farrago exhibiting no logic, no promise, and no manliness. Shrill in its tone, impudent in its ambition. Indeed from the evidence on the page I should say that it is the work of a woman.

SWERDLOW: A woman? Mr Eliot a woman? I knew there was *something.*

STRINDBERG: Undoubtedly a woman – by the name of… What is it, my girl?

ELIOT: *(Utterly betrayed, beginning to sob.)* …Mary Ann Evans.

STRINDBERG: Then I should advise Mary Ann Evans to return to her bonnets and her embroidery, to her powder puffs and pressed flowers, to her husband if she is fortunate enough to have one – considering her lumpen appearance and repellent personality – and leave writing to those of us who understand the art – and the world.

ELIOT sobs softly and helplessly.

SWERDLOW: I must strongly object, Mr Strindberg. The women of today…

STRINDBERG: *(Impatiently.)* Surely we have lavished enough time on this wretched subject. Let us speak at last of my play, *The Dance of Death.*

SWERDLOW: *(Giving in to him.)* Yes… Well, it is growing late. If you have no objection, Mr Eliot? … Miss Evans.

ELIOT: *(With heart-felt sobs.)* But August, you said… We were… You and I on 'The Kugglefryer'… The sunlight of my gaze… Your father's ring… Your mother's nose…

(She snuffles, then controls herself.) Go on, Mrs Swerdlow.

SWERDLOW: Very well.

She flips through her notes.

Then, Mr Strindberg – just one or two points. To begin with, more pauses in your dialogue might be advisable.

STRINDBERG: Pauses?

A long pause.

SWERDLOW: Yes, enigmatic ones preferably, full of mystery. *(A longer pause.)* And menace. Furthermore, I recommend the use of even more non sequiturs. For example…

WORDSWORTH: *(In his sleep, suddenly and loudly.)* Lonely as a cloud! *(He snores.)* Golden daffodils! *(He snores again.)* A jocund company! *(He resumes his slumbers.)*

SWERDLOW: Ah, Mr Wordsworth. *(Pause.)* Mr Wordsworth!

WORDSWORTH: *(Roused from sleep.)* Hmm?

SWERDLOW: Have you something to say? About Mr Strindberg's play?

WORDSWORTH: *(Coming round, now amiable and mellowed by laudanum.)* His play? I see. …Yes, his play. Well, not precisely my sort of thing I suppose. But then, Mr Strindberg seems a truly excellent fellow, a fine writer and a credit to the great country of Sweden. *(Bursting into song.)* 'Sweden forever,/ Kingdom so clever, / Thou art adored / From fjord to shining fjord.' The Swedish national anthem – my own translation. *(Deeply moved.)* My friends, we are all countrymen, all authors, all bards together, serving a great ideal – dedicated to 'a visionary power/ Embodied in the mystery of words,' as I wrote so long ago. *(Loud and amiable again.)* So I say, well done, Mr Strindberg, good on you mate, and Godspeed. *(He yawns.)*

SWERDLOW: Very gracious words, Mr Wordsworth.

STRINDBERG: Very patronising, and strewn with secret meanings. Well, do ask someone else.

SWERDLOW: Certainly. Mr Eliot…Miss Evans. Your views on Mr Strindberg's play?

ELIOT: I… I… *(She tries to speak, but instead begins to sob again.)*

MILNE: Miss Evans…my dear woman…

ELIOT sobs on.

STRINDBERG: Not to worry. Just female problems, that sort of thing. She happened to mention it during the tea break.

MILNE: Did she?

STRINDBERG: And she also gave me her frank appraisal of my play, Mrs Swerdlow. And – as she now seems sadly incapable of expressing these views herself, I'd be happy to pass them on in some detail, if you wish.

SWERDLOW: *(Surprised.)* Would you?

STRINDBERG: Of course. Well then, Miss Evans thinks… What were her exact words? '*The Dance of Death* is an unrivalled masterpiece in the history of dramatic literature – courageous, original, unsentimental. And yet,' she goes on to say, 'it will shock the public with its unconventional structure and horrify with its inconvenient truths. Small minds,' she continues, 'will find it chaotic, harsh and uncompromising, but a few brave souls will cherish it, and a grateful posterity will claim it for its own.' That is the gist of her remarks at any rate.

SWERDLOW: I see. Thank you, Miss Evans.

No reply from the softly weeping ELIOT.

Then, Mr Goethe, would you care to…?

GOETHE: Nein!

SWERDLOW: Ah. In that case… Mr Milne?

MILNE: Thank you. *(Pause.)* Let me say that I found Mr Strindberg's play *The Dance of Death* enchanting and utterly delightful. Madcap, zany, hilarious, sweet-spirited. You have a rare gift, sir.

STRINDBERG: *(Shaken and indignant.)* This is your view? 'Delightful'? 'Sweet'? 'Madcap and zany'?

MILNE: Yes, Mr Strindberg. Absolutely topping. Something for the whole family. Indeed, we acted it out – my dear wifey and I – for the children. Such a relief from the harshness and cynicism of our age.

STRINDBERG: *(Enraged.)* This…to me! To me!

MILNE: It is a soufflé, delicate to the palate, unfraught with weighty ideas or theories, full of divine absurdities, perfectly scrumptious.

STRINDBERG: *(Raving.)* It is an indictment of the universe, of the horror that creeps just beneath the surface of things, of the monster whose spiked back can be seen moving through every act, however generous-seeming or magnanimous. It reveals at a stroke the perfidy of woman, the fraud of family ties, the hypocrisy of the bourgeoisie, the dark insidiousness of the working classes, the malignity of nature.

MILNE:	And such slapstick! Every time the Captain collapsed, my dear wife and I hooted with delight – as did the little ones – Christopher Robin, Elizabeth Skylark and little Belinda Crested Grebe. Even the baby gurgled with pleasure, rolling about in her pram in an ecstasy of merriment. A joyous family scene; it would have touched your heart.
STRINDBERG:	This to me! To me? *(He growls in fury. Then, in alarm.)* Aaah! My head! My head!
	Moaning, STRINDBERG collapses in his chair, slumping forward, and is silent. The others look on in surprise. A pause.
SWERDLOW:	Mr Strindberg? Are you quite…?
	STRINDBERG comes round, slowly sitting up again.
SWERDLOW:	Ah, he's reviving.
STRINDBERG:	*(Growling.)* What happened?
SWERDLOW:	You passed out, Mr Strindberg. Are you all right?
STRINDBERG:	Fine, fine. Never better. *(Darkly suspicious.)* What exactly took place while I was unconscious? *(To ELIOT.)* Where you unfaithful to me?
ELIOT:	*(Shocked.)* What?
STRINDBERG:	I see it in your eyes, hard-hearted vixen! You had sexual relations, did you not…with A A Milne?
MILNE:	*(Gallantly.)* Mr Eliot was a perfect lady during the entire length of your seizure, sir.
ELIOT:	Thank you, Mr Milne. *(Boldly.)* And as for you, Mr Strindberg, I wish to announce that, as of this moment, we are no longer betrothed. I will not accept your ring. I am calling off our engagement.

STRINDBERG:	Demon! Vampire! To be treated like this! No one knows how I suffer! No one cares! *(He growls a bit more.)*
	Pause.
SWERDLOW:	*(As sunnily as the circumstances permit.)* Well, I think we'd best hurry along now. So little time. Mr Goethe, let us talk about your *Faust*.
GOETHE:	Nein!
SWERDLOW:	*(Wearily.)* 'Nein'?
GOETHE:	*(Slight but unmistakable German accent.)* Nein. I do not wish to discuss it, Frau Swerdlow. *Faust* is no more. I have destroyed the manuscript, and I urge all of you to destroy your copies as well.
SWERDLOW:	*(Shocked.)* But why, Mr Goethe?
GOETHE:	I have come to the realisation, Frau Swerdlow, that it is a complete failure. Indeed, for all that I have ever written and for all that I might ever write I have nothing but scorn, withering scorn and mocking contempt. I shall write no more. I shall write no more.
SWERDLOW:	*(Greatly concerned.)* Mr Goethe…
GOETHE:	At first I considered killing myself in the German Romantic manner which has served my country so well over the years. But at that moment I was unable to find my pistol amidst the great voluminous folds of my swirling black cloak. Then I thought: no, I shall not end my life, I shall change it, change it utterly. I shall become…a shepherd, a simple shepherd, piping to my flock, my faithful dog Strudel beside me. Or perhaps a trapeze artist in twinkling sequinned tights and a bandana – 'The Great Mendoza' – idol of the cheering throng.

Or, on the other hand, I could become…a Pilgrim for Truth, a lonely wanderer through picturesque landscapes, often seen from behind as I gaze into a sea of clouds from some lofty promontory, the eagles crying above me. *(Thoughtfully.)* Not an easy choice, my friends.

SWERDLOW: But why?…

GOETHE: Why am I abandoning the literary life? I read everything submitted for today's workshop, Frau Swerdlow, and found one piece of writing to be a gigantic, peerless masterwork, a composition of sublime and incredible genius. I myself could never hope to equal, nay to approach the achievement of one of our number. I now see that, like my Faust, I have lusted after a glory that could never be mine. So I wish to convey my congratulations, indeed my homage to Herr Milne for his story, 'Piglet Meets a Heffalump'. There is grandeur in this deceptively simple tale, my friends; there is elegance and subtlety and truth, and an understanding of the human dilemma that fills the heart with wisdom and wonder.

MILNE: Very kind of you to say so, Mr Goethe. But your *Faust* is a charming thing. Hours and hours and *hours* of pleasure.

GOETHE: Please, Herr Milne. I am unworthy of your praise. Though your generosity of soul, sir, does not surprise me. It is evident in each word of the narrative, in each line spoken by Pooh and Piglet, and in the architecture and scope of the great story itself, which is – let us face it – the story of us all, in every land and every age.

MILNE: But Mr Goethe…

GOETHE: For who among us, my friends, is not seeking his own Heffalump? Indeed, who is not, in some strange way, a Heffalump himself? And yet who is not, in truth, not a Heffalump? And yet the Heffalump himself does not exist, he is not, and therefore he alone is, is he not? Or is he? Or, for that matter, was he ever? *(He shakes his head.)* Teasing questions for our times.

SWERDLOW: Yes, quite…

GOETHE: *(Expansively.)* A Titan stands among us, my friends, like a great immemorial oak, and we shrivel in his shadow like mere flowers of a day – like your 'Daffodils' Herr Wordsworth, your novel Frau Evans, your play Herr Strindberg, and my own feeble *Faust*. Out of respect for the art I love, I shall disgrace it no longer, and I suggest that you all consider your positions as well. Write no more, I counsel you. Write no more.

ELIOT: *(Despondently.)* No more?

GOETHE: It is futile to continue. Vain presumption.

MILNE: But my dear chap…

GOETHE: *(Sadly and resolutely.)* Nein, Herr Milne. Nein. *(He sighs deeply.)*

Pause. ELIOT, STRINDBERG and WORDSWORTH seem depressed.

SWERDLOW: *(Taken aback, and seeking to rally spirits.)* Well, thank you, Mr Goethe for your observations. And yet, I'm sure there is no need for you – for any of you – to give up your writing.

(With desperate enthusiasm.) No, on the contrary, you must persevere as never before. Next week when you return to the workshop, you will have rewritten your contributions, Mr Wordsworth, Miss Evans

and Mr Strindberg, in the light of what you have learned – of what we have all learned – here today. But as for you, Mr Goethe, as you seem determined not to continue with your *Faust*, for next week I want you to unleash your imagination in an entirely different direction. I've been making notes… *(She holds up some papers.)* …about a quite new idea for you. A book, Mr Goethe, a self-help manual.

GOETHE: Ja?

SWERDLOW: Ja! A confidence-building guide to life, rich with advice and encouragement, inspiring your readers to overcome their doubts and fears and gloomy speculations and to achieve their own desired goals. You could include brief biographies of great men and women who have striven bravely against enormous odds. I think I may be able to persuade the St Ubalda Press to show some interest. I promise you, Mr Goethe, that such a project will benefit not only others, but yourself as well. *(Grandly.)* You could call it simply, 'The Indomitable Human Spirit'.

Bang! A pistol shot. GOETHE grunts in pain, slumps forward, and falls to the floor, the pistol still in his hand.

SWERDLOW: Mr Goethe!

ELIOT: *(Alarmed and sobbing again.)* Mr Goethe! Mr Goethe!

WORDSWORTH: Shot himself!

MILNE: Oh, my dear dear fellow!

Pause, as they all observe the fallen GOETHE at a distance.

ELIOT: Do you think…he's dead, Mrs Swerdlow?

SWERDLOW: It seems likely. In addition to being a poet, dramatist, novelist, philosopher, critic and scientist – as well as optician, tree surgeon, skiing instructor and the finest ventriloquist of his generation – Mr Goethe was a superb marksman, the greatest in all Germany, so they say.

ELIOT: *(Sorrowfully.)* I see.

SWERDLOW: And at such close range, he could hardly…

The DOCTOR bursts into the room, carrying a small black case. He is the man with the trim beard who had entered by mistake at the opening of the play.

DOCTOR: *(Slavic accent.)* Pardon me. I heard a pistol-shot, and I wondered if I could be of assistance. I am a doctor.

SWERDLOW: Are you? Yes, please. Over there, Dr…

DOCTOR: Dr Chekhov. *(Establishing his credentials.)* M.B., Moscow University; PhD., Odessa Polytechnic. I'm taking a brush-up course on the pancreas here at West Bromley, just across the corridor. *(Solemnly.)* I'll…have a look.

He goes and examines GOETHE at some length, as the others venture slightly nearer.

He's gone, I'm afraid. Bullet through the heart, poor devil.

ELIOT sobs anew, MILNE sighs sadly.

Suicide, I shouldn't be surprised. Gun in his hand, scornful smile on his lips. *(Pause.)* Was he a German Romantic poet, by any chance?

SWERDLOW: Indeed he was, Doctor.

DOCTOR: *(Knowingly.)* Ah, yes. *(With interest, glancing about.)* I say, is this the writers' workshop?

SWERDLOW:	Yes, Doctor. *(With interest.)* Are you yourself a…writer?
DOCTOR:	I dabble. Short stories, farces, melancholy comedies. Often about doctors – and landowners, serfs, soldiers, students…
SWERDLOW:	*(Hopefully.)* 'Surfers', did you say?
DOCTOR:	No, 'serfs'. The land-working peasantry of old Russia.
SWERDLOW:	*(Disappointed.)* I see. Not much demand for that sort of thing these days. But come and join us next week, why don't you? – we have a vacancy at the moment – and bring along some of your work. Perhaps we can extend your range.
DOCTOR:	Thank you, I will. And now, if you'll excuse me, madam, I must contact the proper authorities – about the corpse. Dosvedanya.
SWERDLOW:	Goodbye, Dr Check-up.

The DOCTOR exits. MRS SWERDLOW returns to her desk.

SWERDLOW:	And of course I look forward to seeing all of <u>you</u> next week as well. *(Pause. Then, apprehensively.)* Mr Wordsworth.

WORDSWORTH sits gloomily for a moment, then takes a final slug of laudanum and sinks into oblivion, snoring.

SWERDLOW:	*(Anxiously.)* Miss Evans.
ELIOT:	I… I'm afraid I…

She resumes weeping wearily.

SWERDLOW:	*(More anxiously.)* Mr Strindberg.
STRINDBERG:	*(Growling.)* To me. This, to me! *(In alarm.)* Aaah!

He clutches his head and collapses in his chair as before, and is silent. No one seems to notice.

SWERDLOW: *(Almost desperately.)* Mr Milne?

MILNE: Of course, Mrs Swerdlow. Indeed I've
             just had an idea for a new story based on
             something the late Mr Goethe said – about
             my being like a great oak-tree. Pooh-bear
             climbs an oak in the middle of the forest to
             steal some honey, but a branch breaks and
             he tumbles down as the bees go, 'Buzz, buzz,
             buzz!' *(He sighs with delight.)* I'll write it all up
             and bring it along next week. And I do so
             look forward to hearing your views on it, my
             friends – such a valuable process.

SWERDLOW: *(Highly relieved.)* So, Mr Milne, you feel that
             today has been a rewarding experience?

MILNE: Most certainly, Mrs Swerdlow. Quite
             marvellous. Unmissable. Memorable.
             Inspiring. Tremendous. *(A pause. Then, with
             great exuberance.)* Absolutely topping.

             *MILNE stands, a radiant figure, amidst the snoring
             WORDSWORTH, the weeping ELIOT, the fainted
             STRINDBERG and the dead GOETHE. MRS SWERDLOW
             looks on with satisfaction.*

             Curtain

BY THE SAME AUTHOR

Codpieces
9781849430555

'To be or not to be?' may be The Question, but it is not the only one. *Hamlet, Part II*, for example, answers a question about *Hamlet* that has plagued scholars, readers and play-goers for over four hundred years: What happened next? *Prince Lear* tackles yet another conundrum: What happened just before the start of *King Lear*, setting in motion the improbable events of Act I, scene 1? And in *Fatal Loins*, the question answered by the play is directly posed in the prologue: *'If Juliet and Romeo survive / Will their eternal passion stay alive?'*

'I am no stranger to Shakespearean parody…but reading Pontac I am (only slightly) mortified to find that he can write cod Shakespeare much better than Peter Cook, Jonathan Miller, Dudley Moore or myself.' – Alan Bennett, from the Foreword

'Perfect if you want something intelligent and hilarious to stage, perhaps with students. Each play is an accomplished, laugh-aloud Shakespeare parody.' Susan Elkin, *The Stage*

'Highly amusing… These works may be short, clearly designed to fit into a slot in 30 minutes or so, but the quality of the writing and intelligence of the playwright shines through… It is greatly to be hoped that a stage producer decides to take an option on these plays, as well as commissioning many more since they would surely delight any discerning theatrical audience.' British Theatre Guide

'a phenomenally intelligent and perfectly crafted trio of Shakespeare parodies. A delightfully witty and entertaining collection.' *Buzz Magazine*

WWW.OBERONBOOKS.COM

 Follow us on www.twitter.com/@oberonbooks
& www.facebook.com/oberonbook